the
PIE
project

the PIE project

by PHOEBE WOOD and KIRSTEN JENKINS

hardie grant books

CONTENTS

INTRODUCTION

Phoebe My obsession with pies began during a three-month trip to New York City almost three years ago. In desperate need for a change, I had quit my job, packed up my life and travelled to a city that I had never been to and where I barely knew a soul. I spent those three months exploring any and every part of the city I happened to end up in that day. Ten kilos (twenty-two pounds) later, I had well and truly eaten my fair share of pies (oh, and doughnuts) and had a crack at making my own on my first Thanksgiving (it was pecan and chocolate, thank you!).

It's hard to put my finger on why pies struck such a special chord with me, but I just loved how 'pie' had a real culture in the States. It seemed to me like it was something that everyone knew how to make over there, and everyone had a family recipe or a favourite filling they would recommend. Blogs, websites and cookbooks recite the history of pies and record thousands of attempts at 'the perfect crust'. There are entire shops, such as the Four and Twenty Blackbirds pie shop in New York, solely devoted to selling their single product: pie. And Christina Tosi's Crack Pie has a cult following all around the world! Pie was a revelation to me.

When I came home to Sydney, I spent months perfecting the art of the pie crust, which was so different from the style of pastry I was used to making. Pie pastry is rich with thick chunks of good-quality butter, and it usually has a little vinegar added to it to prevent gluten-strands from forming, resulting in a perfectly flaky, crunchy crust. Weekends were consumed in pursuit of pie perfection and new filling combinations, much to the delight of my friends and family. It was on a Sunday when the idea struck me: I *had* to write a book about pies. Who could I convince to do it with me? Only one person came to mind.

Kirsten Even before meeting Phoebe I had heard everything about her! We were only a couple of years apart at TAFE (college) and had the same teachers there. We started at two different food magazines at the same time and the food industry is so small we knew all the same people. Only we had never met. Our paths finally crossed when Phoebe came home from New York to work on SBS's *Feast* magazine, where at the time I was freelancing. We instantly hit it off with our first phone conversation consisting of only laughter (and a bit about food)! We had, and still have, the same philosophy when it comes to food. It was so nice finding someone on that same page.

Phoebe: When people meet Kirsten, they suffer what I like to call 'the Kirsten effect'. She's good at just about everything, but when it comes to styling, she takes things to another level. I've learned so much from her and we are constantly challenging each other to be better. The fact that she happens to be pretty handy with a camera is a bonus. My proposal was via text and read something like, 'Hey, how would you feel about shooting a cookbook?' and she instantly wrote back: 'Yes.' From the beginning, Kirsten was my constant motivation for making this project the absolute best it could be.

Kirsten: This was a pretty easy proposition: come up with a dream vision of what you want your book to look like, collect props, choose backgrounds and construct graphic images that reflect both of your personalities.

Both: This book is all about experimentation, appreciation and enjoyment. No matter how many times you make a pie, it is always different. One day it's a sugary jam explosion; the next day it's the flakiest crust you've ever eaten. We want people to feel fearless and confident when they cut the butter through their first pastry. We want people to experience the wonderful anticipation and joy of baking and know that no result will be bad, just different. This is not a book about French patisserie or fine-dining desserts, these are just really good recipes for the home cook to blow the socks off their friends and family. This book is about a project that we really believe in and is wholly ours: our vision and recipes, our triumphs and failures. Our friends and family were our taste testers, our critics and our supporters, and we received looks of awe, elation and some definite looks of confusion (those ones didn't make it in, we promise). We truly hope that every pie you make will tell a new story, and you make it your own personal pie project.

Rhubarb, strawberry, balsamic and thyme pie

My mum used to make a killer retro salad: strawberries, baby spinach and balsamic vinegar. I loved it. The sweetness of the summer strawberries blended with the balsamic vinegar to make a tart salad dressing. It was really kitsch but I thought it was great when it got rolled out for summer barbecues. The same combination works just as well in this pie, especially with the addition of strawberries' best friend, rhubarb. – *Kirsten*

Serves 8

2 × 435 g (15½ oz) frozen Careme vanilla bean pastry, thawed, or other bought sweet shortcrust rolled to a thickness of 3 mm (⅛ in)

1 kg (2 lb 3 oz) rhubarb, trimmed and cut into 5 cm (2 in) pieces

1 vanilla bean, split lengthways and seeds scraped

220 g (8 oz) caster (superfine) sugar

3 thyme sprigs

2 teaspoons cornflour (cornstarch)

500 g (1 lb 2 oz) strawberries, hulled and halved

2 tablespoons balsamic vinegar

1 egg, lightly beaten

1 tablespoon demerara sugar, for sprinkling

Preheat the oven to 180°C (350°F). Line a 20 cm (8 in) pie dish with one of the pastry sheets, leaving a 1 cm (½ in) overhang. Line the pastry case with baking paper, fill with baking beads (or uncooked rice or dried beans) and bake for 15 minutes or until the pastry is just dry and light golden. Remove the paper and baking beads and leave to cool. Cut the remaining pastry sheet into eight 4 cm (1½ in) strips. Chill the strips while you make the filling.

Cook the rhubarb, vanilla, caster sugar and thyme sprigs with 60 ml (2 fl oz/¼ cup) of water in a large deep frying pan over medium heat. Carefully stir until the sugar starts to dissolve, then reduce the heat to medium–low, cover and simmer for 8 minutes or until the rhubarb is almost tender. Using a slotted spoon, transfer the rhubarb to a colander set over a bowl and discard the thyme sprigs. Leave to drain very well.

Combine the rhubarb syrup with the cornflour and return to the pan set over medium heat. Boil for 10 minutes or until thick and syrupy then leave to cool for 10 minutes.

Carefully fold the rhubarb through the syrup followed by the strawberries and balsamic vinegar. Spread the cooled filling into the pastry case.

Make a lattice top with the cooled strips (see page 150) and place it over the filling. Trim any excess, pinching the edges to seal. Brush with the beaten egg and sprinkle with the demerara sugar. Place on a baking tray and bake for 55 minutes or until golden. Rest for 30 minutes before serving.

Pear, maple syrup and brown butter pies with cinnamon spelt crust

This recipe changed my step-father's life! Glenny – or as we refer to each other 'Steppy' – is married to my mum, who is one impressive woman. The one little issue with my mum, Debs, is she is a complete health nut and her idea of a dessert is a blended avocado mousse. So someone needs to look after Steppy in the dessert department and bring him a bit of joy. After photographing this recipe for the book, I packed it up and smuggled it into a family dinner for Steppy. I told him to have a small piece that night and then hide the rest for treats later in the week. One problem: the rest of the extended family got wind of Steppy's 'special' dessert and he was left with barely enough to get him through the next day. – Kirsten

Serves 12
Makes 2 × 23 cm × 10 cm (9 in × 4 in) pies

3 hard, crisp pears, e.g. Beurré Bosc pears, peeled

250 g (9 oz/1 cup) dark muscovado sugar

250 ml (8½ fl oz/1 cup) maple syrup

thick cream, to serve

Spelt pastry

400 g (14 oz/2⅔ cups) spelt flour

2 teaspoons ground cinnamon

115 g (4 oz/½ cup) caster (superfine) sugar

½ teaspoon fine sea salt

250 g (9 oz) cold unsalted butter, chopped

2 tablespoons apple cider vinegar mixed with 125 ml (4 fl oz/½ cup) cold water and 4 ice cubes

Brown butter custard

120 g (4½ oz) unsalted butter

1 vanilla bean, split lengthways and seeds scraped

2 eggs

110 g (4 oz) caster (superfine) sugar

50 g (1¾ oz/⅓ cup) plain (all-purpose) flour

For the spelt pastry, combine the flour, cinnamon, sugar and salt in a bowl. Add the butter pieces and toss to coat. Turn out onto a clean work surface and, using a pastry cutter (or flat-bladed knife), roughly cut the butter into the flour. Make a well in the centre and gradually add the vinegar water in 3 batches, mixing together with your hands, until a coarse dough forms. Divide in half, shape into discs and wrap in plastic wrap. Chill for at least 3 hours.

Working with one piece of pastry at a time, roll out each piece on a lightly floured work surface to 32 cm × 17 cm (12¾ in × 6¾ in). Use to line two 23 cm × 10 cm (9 in × 4 in) pie dishes. Trim the edges to neaten, but allow some excess to overhang the sides. Chill for 1 hour.

For the pear filling, place the pears, muscovado sugar, maple syrup and 1.25 litres (42 fl oz/ 5 cups) of water in a saucepan set over medium–low heat. Cover with a cartouche (a circle of baking paper) and bring to a simmer. Reduce the heat to low and cook gently for 1 hour or until the syrup is dark golden and the pears are tender. Let the pears cool in the syrup, then remove the pears from the syrup and simmer 250 ml (8½ fl oz/1 cup) of the syrup in a saucepan over high heat for 15 minutes or until thickened. Leave to cool.

Preheat the oven to 200°C (400°F). Line the two pie dishes with baking paper and baking beads (or uncooked rice or dried beans) and blind bake for 15 minutes or until the edges are just dry. Remove the beads and paper and bake the cases for a further 5 minutes or until the bases are just dry. Leave to cool completely. Reduce the oven temperature to 160°C (320°F).

To make the brown butter custard, melt the butter in a saucepan over medium–high heat for 6 minutes or until it is nut brown. Add the vanilla seeds and remove from the heat. Whisk the eggs and sugar together in a bowl, then whisk the butter mixture into the egg mixture to combine. Whisk in the flour until smooth. Divide between the cooled pastry cases.

Thickly slice the pears and arrange in the pastry cases, allowing the pears to rest on top of the custard. Bake for 20 minutes or until the custard is just set. Remove from the oven and cool to room temperature. Drizzle with the thickened pear syrup and serve with thick cream.

Blueberry and lavender pie with hazelnut crust

Unless someone stopped me I would try and put lavender in most desserts (lucky that Phoebe is here to stop me!). It's not a 'herb' that you see used every day and if it's not used with restraint it can really taste like a potpourri sachet. Thankfully we did show restraint in this recipe and the combination of the blueberry, lavender and the earthy crust is just right. Make sure to use an edible variety of lavender. – *Kirsten*

Serves 8

500 g (1 lb 2 oz) frozen or fresh blueberries

170 g (6 oz/³/₄ cup) caster (superfine) sugar

1 tablespoon cornflour (cornstarch)

1 teaspoon crushed dried edible lavender

2 teaspoons vanilla bean paste

Hazelnut pastry

250 g (9 oz/1²/₃ cups) hazelnuts, finely ground

100 g (3¹/₂ oz/²/₃ cup) gluten-free plain (all-purpose) flour

75 g (2³/₄ oz) caster (superfine) sugar

1 egg, lightly beaten with 1 tablespoon water

Preheat the oven to 180°C (350°F). For the hazelnut pastry, combine all the ingredients in a bowl to make a thick nutty paste. Using your hands, press the mixture into the base and side of a 21 cm (8¹/₄ in) pie dish. Bake for 10 minutes or until just dry then remove from the oven and leave to cool.

Cook the blueberries and sugar in a saucepan over high heat, stirring, for 10 minutes or until syrupy. Remove from the heat and mix the cornflour with 4 tablespoons of the blueberry mixture in a bowl until smooth. Stir the thickened cornflour into the rest of the blueberry mixture along with the lavender. Cook for 5 minutes over low heat or until thickened. Cool slightly, then pour into the crust and place on a baking tray. Cook for 30 minutes until bubbling and jammy. Rest for 30 minutes before serving.

Grape, honey and mascarpone galette

This is one of my favourite recipes in the book. The honey and mascarpone cooks to a soft-baked custard, and the grapes burst gently into it. You can eat it warm from the oven, or rest it and allow it to cool and set to a firmer custard. As soon as we finished shooting this, Kirsten told me she hated cooked grapes in desserts. Luckily, I think I changed her mind. – Phoebe

Serves 8

750 g (1 lb 11 oz) mascarpone cheese

115 g (4 oz/^{1}/$_3$ cup) honey

30 g (1 oz/^{1}/$_4$ cup) cornflour (cornstarch)

1 teaspoon vanilla bean paste

300 g (10^1/$_2$ oz) seedless red grapes

2 tablespoons caster (superfine) sugar

Pastry

200 g (7 oz/1^1/$_3$ cups) plain (all-purpose) flour

55 g (2 oz/^{1}/$_4$ cup) caster (superfine) sugar

^{1}/$_4$ teaspoon fine sea salt

125 g (4^1/$_2$ oz) unsalted butter, chopped

2 teaspoons apple cider vinegar mixed with 80 ml (2^1/$_2$ fl oz/^{1}/$_3$ cup) cold water and 4 ice cubes

For the pastry, combine the flour, sugar and salt in a bowl. Add the butter pieces and toss to coat. Turn out onto a clean work surface and, using a pastry cutter (or flat-bladed knife), roughly cut the butter into the flour (leave some large chunks of butter in the mixture, as this will ensure the pastry becomes nice and flaky as it cooks).

Make a well in the centre of the flour mixture and add the vinegar water in 3 batches, using your hands to fold it into the flour to combine. Shape into a disc, wrap in plastic wrap and chill for 3 hours.

Roll out the chilled pastry on a lightly floured work surface to a circle with the thickness of 3 mm (^{1}/$_8$ in). Lay inside a 24 cm × 5 cm deep (9^1/$_2$ in × 2 in) pie dish or ovenproof frying pan and chill for 30 minutes.

Preheat the oven to 200°C (400°F). Whisk the mascarpone, honey and cornflour in a saucepan over medium–low heat for 5 minutes or until smooth and combined. Transfer to a bowl and cool to room temperature. Stir through the vanilla bean paste. Toss the grapes and sugar together in a bowl.

When the mascarpone mixture has cooled, pour into the pastry case and bring the edge up to cover the filling by about 1–2 cm (^{1}/$_2$–^{3}/$_4$ in). Bake for 15 minutes or until the mascarpone is starting to set. Remove from the oven and top with the sugared grapes. Bake for a further 30 minutes or until the pastry is golden and cooked and the mascarpone has set. Rest for 30 minutes before serving for a soft set custard, or cool completely for a firmer custard.

Peach, white chocolate and bourbon slab pie

Peaches, to me, are the ultimate taste of childhood and remind me of summers with my sisters Grace and Ali, on my parents' stone fruit orchard in Barry, plucking them straight off the tree and eating them with the juices dribbling down our arms. – Phoebe

Serves 18

2.5 kg (5½ lb) peaches, stones removed, peeled and chopped

300 g (11 oz) caster (superfine) sugar

2 vanilla beans, split lengthways and seeds scraped

60 ml (2 fl oz/¼ cup) bourbon

200 g (7 oz) white chocolate, chopped

3 teaspoons cornflour (cornstarch)

1 egg, beaten

2 tablespoons demerara sugar, for sprinkling

Pastry

400 g (14 oz/2⅔ cups) plain (all-purpose) flour

55 g (2 oz/¼ cup) caster (superfine) sugar

½ teaspoon fine sea salt

250 g (9 oz) cold unsalted butter, cut into 2 cm (¾ in) cubes

2 tablespoons apple cider vinegar mixed with 125 ml (4 fl oz/½ cup) cold water and 4 ice cubes

For the pastry, combine the flour, sugar and salt in a bowl. Add the butter pieces and toss to coat. Turn out onto a clean work surface and, using a pastry cutter (or flat-bladed knife), roughly cut the butter into the flour mixture (leave some large chunks of butter as this will help the pastry to become nice and flaky as it cooks).

Create a well in the centre of the flour mixture and add the vinegar water in 3 batches, working it in with your hands to form a rough dough (you may not need all the water). Divide the dough into 2 pieces, one twice the size of the other. Shape into discs, wrap in plastic wrap and chill for 3 hours.

Cook the peaches, caster sugar, vanilla seeds and pods in a large saucepan over medium–low heat, stirring often, for 1 hour 20 minutes, until thick and jammy. Remove from the heat, stir in the bourbon, then cool. Fold in the chocolate and cornflour.

Roll out the larger piece of pastry on a lightly floured work surface to a thickness of 3 mm (⅛ in) and use it to line the base of a 40 cm × 30 cm × 7 cm (16 in × 12 in × 2¾ in) baking dish. Roll out the second, smaller piece of pastry to 40 cm × 30 cm (16 in × 12 in) and place on a baking tray lined with baking paper. Make small crosses in the second sheet and chill both sheets for 30 minutes.

Preheat the oven to 200°C (400°F). Spread the pastry case with the jammy mixture, then cover with the second sheet of pastry and fold over the edges of the first sheet to enclose. Brush with the beaten egg and scatter with demerara sugar. Bake for 20 minutes, then reduce the oven temperature to 180°C (350°F) and bake for 40 minutes or until the pastry is crisp and golden. Rest for 30 minutes before serving.

Golden syrup and chocolate pecan pies

I grew up by the beaches in Sydney and my two loves were surfing and surf club, and food. I joined Wanda Surf Club when I was seven and took part in races up until I was 22; every summer weekend was all about being down at the beach and being in the water. When we'd left the beach after surfing for the day, it was all about what I was going to eat. One day when I was about 11, my coach Jeff 'Charlie' Brown brought those two loves of mine together. Being totally aware of the incredible nerves I suffered before a race, he did something that completely distracted me: he said to me, 'If you win this today, I will buy you a whole pecan pie that you don't have to share with anyone else.' Well, I was so determined to win that pie (not really the race) that I went out there . . . and won the pie. To this day I could eat a whole pecan pie if you gave it to me, and this golden syrup and chocolate pecan pie proved very hard to walk away from. – Kirsten

Serves 12
Makes 2 × 20 cm (8 in) pies

2 × 300 g (10½ oz) frozen Careme chocolate pastry, thawed, or other bought chocolate shortcrust rolled to a thickness of 3 mm (⅛ in)

250 g (9 oz) soft brown sugar

350 g (12½ oz/1 cup) golden syrup

80 g (2¾ oz) unsalted butter

2 teaspoons natural vanilla extract

80 ml (2½ fl oz/⅓ cup) pouring (single/light) cream

1 teaspoon ground allspice

3 eggs

350 g (12½ oz) toasted pecans, chopped

100 g (3½ oz) dark chocolate, chopped

Preheat the oven to 180°C (350°F). Line two 20 cm (8 in) shallow pie dishes with the pastry and trim the edges to neaten. Line the pastry cases with baking paper and fill with baking beads (or uncooked rice or dried beans). Bake for 15 minutes or until the pastry is just dry to the touch. Remove the paper and baking beads and leave to cool. Reduce the oven temperature to 160°C (320°F).

Gently cook the sugar, golden syrup, butter, vanilla, cream and allspice in a saucepan over low heat for 4 minutes, stirring to dissolve the sugar. Remove from the heat and beat in the eggs, one at a time. Leave to cool, then stir through the chopped pecans and the chopped chocolate.

Divide evenly between the two pastry cases and bake for 35 minutes or until set on the edges but with a gentle wobble in the centre. Cool to room temperature before serving.

Rhubarb, rosewater and spelt pie

Rhubarb is the ultimate pie fruit (although, technically, it is actually a vegetable). It goes with citrus, berries, custard, cream, hot, cold – it doesn't seem to matter what you do with it, it always works. I love rhubarb for its tart flavour and jammy texture when cooked, and in this recipe it's made extra-earthy with a buttery spelt pastry. And I do a pretty good job of convincing myself that spelt also makes it kind of healthy. Kind of. – Phoebe

Serves 8

1 kg (2 lb 3 oz) rhubarb, chopped

220 g (8 oz) caster (superfine) sugar

1 tablespoon rosewater

1½ tablespoons cornflour (cornstarch)

1 egg, lightly beaten

1 tablespoon demerara sugar

Pastry

375 g (13 oz/2½ cups) plain (all-purpose) spelt flour

55 g (2 oz/¼ cup) caster (superfine) sugar

½ teaspoon fine sea salt

250 g (9 oz) cold unsalted butter, cut into 2 cm (¾ in) pieces

2 tablespoons apple cider vinegar mixed with 125 ml (4 fl oz/½ cup) cold water and 4 ice cubes

For the pastry, combine the flour, sugar and salt in a bowl. Add the butter pieces and toss to coat. Turn out onto a clean work surface and, using a pastry cutter (or flat-bladed knife), roughly cut the butter into the flour mixture (leave some large chunks of butter as this will help the pastry to become nice and flaky as it cooks).

Create a well in the centre of the flour mixture and add the vinegar water in 3 batches, working it in with your hands to form a rough dough (you may not need all of the water). Divide the dough in half, shape each piece into a rough disc and wrap in plastic wrap. Chill for 3 hours.

Cook the rhubarb and caster sugar with 2 tablespoons of water in a saucepan over medium heat, stirring occasionally, for 15 minutes or until the rhubarb is thick and jammy. Stir through the rosewater and cornflour and set aside to cool completely.

When the pastry has chilled, roll each piece out on a lightly floured work surface into a circle with a thickness of 3 mm (⅛ in). Use one pastry circle to line the base and side of a 24 cm (9½ in) pie dish, and place the other on a baking tray lined with baking paper. Chill both for 30 minutes.

Preheat the oven to 180°C (350°F). Spoon the cooled rhubarb mixture into the pastry-lined pie dish. Cut seven 1.5 cm (½ in) circles from the pastry circle and lay the lid over the filling. Trim off the excess pastry, pinching the edges to seal. Brush the beaten egg over the top and sprinkle with the demerara sugar. Place on a baking tray and bake for 55 minutes or until golden and the filling is bubbling and jammy. Rest for 30 minutes before serving.

Blueberry, pear and lemon pie

Our Christmas summer holiday last year consisted of long hot days on Mollymook Beach on the south coast of New South Wales. Surfing, swimming, eating and sleeping. This program of daily events was interrupted only by one day of quite overcast weather when we decided to visit the berry farm just a bit further down the coast. After a slightly rough off-road adventure (in a not so suitable car) we arrived at a hidden oasis in the middle of what seemed like nowhere. We picked enough buckets of blueberries to keep several families supplied for the holidays! After eating our weight in blueberries, we decided to freeze the leftovers to use throughout the coming year. So I'm excited to say, the bubbly lattice pie that sits in front of you was produced solely from those summer berry pickings. – Kirsten

Serves 8

1 kg (2 lb 3 oz) fresh or frozen blueberries

3 hard, crisp pears, e.g. Beurré Bosc pears, peeled and chopped into 2 cm (³/₄ in) pieces

220 g (8 oz) caster (superfine) sugar

1 vanilla bean, split lengthways and seeds scraped

finely grated zest of 1 lemon

3 teaspoons cornflour (cornstarch)

1 egg, lightly beaten with 1 tablespoon water

1 tablespoon demerara sugar

<u>Pastry</u>

375 g (13 oz/2¹/₂ cups) plain (all-purpose) flour

55 g (2 oz/¹/₄ cup) caster (superfine) sugar

¹/₂ teaspoon fine sea salt

250 g (9 oz) cold unsalted butter, cut into 2 cm (³/₄ in) pieces

2 tablespoons apple cider vinegar mixed with 125 ml (4 fl oz /¹/₂ cup) cold water and 4 ice cubes

For the pastry, combine the flour, sugar and salt in a bowl. Add the butter pieces and toss to coat. Turn out onto a clean work surface and, using a pastry cutter (or flat-bladed knife), roughly cut the butter into the flour mixture (leave some large chunks of butter as this will help the pastry to become nice and flaky as it cooks).

Create a well in the centre of the flour mixture and add the vinegar water in 3 batches, working it in with your hands to form a rough dough (you may not need all of the water). Divide the dough in half, shape each piece into a rough disc and wrap in plastic wrap. Chill for 3 hours.

Working with one piece of pastry at a time, roll out on a lightly floured work surface to a thickness of 3 mm (¹/₈ in) thick. Use the first pastry sheet to line the base and side of a 23 cm × 4 cm deep (9 in × 1¹/₂ in) pie dish, leaving a 3 cm (1¹/₄ in) overhang. Roll out the second piece of pastry to a thickness of 3 mm (¹/₈ in) and cut into eight 3 cm (1¹/₄ in) wide strips. Chill both for 1 hour.

For the blueberry filling, heat the blueberries, pear, caster sugar, vanilla seeds and lemon zest in a large saucepan over medium–low heat. Cook, stirring occasionally, for 25 minutes until syrupy. Put the cornflour in a bowl and combine with 3 tablespoons of the blueberry liquid. Stir until smooth. Return to the pan and cook for a further 5 minutes until thickened. Remove from the heat and leave to cool completely.

Preheat the oven to 200°C (400°F). Place the lined pie dish on a baking tray and fill with the blueberry mixture. Make a lattice top with the chilled strips (see page 150), place it over the filling and press to seal. Trim off any excess pastry from the strips, then fold over the overhanging pastry to conceal the ends of the lattice strips and to seal. Brush with the egg wash, scatter with demerara sugar and bake for 20 minutes or until the pastry is turning a golden colour. Reduce the oven temperature to 180°C (350°F) and cook for a further 40 minutes or until the pastry is crisp and golden, and the filling is bubbling. Rest for 30 minutes before serving.

Spiced apple and golden syrup pie

This pie reminds me of a really good British pudding, a great one you get from a proper pub lunch. The apples are slightly spiced and are rich and sweet with the toffee flavour of golden syrup, and it is topped with crisp buttery bread – think a crispy bread and butter pudding. – Kirsten

Serves 8

150 g (5½ oz) unsalted butter

1.5 kg (3 lb 5 oz) apples, peeled, cored and roughly chopped

110 g (4 oz) caster (superfine) sugar

250 g (9 oz) golden syrup

½ teaspoon ground cardamom

1½ teaspoons ground allspice

300 ml (10 fl oz) thick (double/heavy) cream

1 teaspoon natural vanilla extract

1 loaf pane di casa, crusts removed, torn into 1 cm (½ in) and 2 cm (¾ in) pieces (550 g/1 lb 3 oz crumbs)

100 g (3½ oz/1 cup) pecans, chopped

½ teaspoon fine sea salt

vanilla ice cream to serve

Pastry

200 g (7 oz/1⅓ cups) plain (all-purpose) flour

¼ teaspoon fine sea salt

55 g (2 oz/¼ cup) caster (superfine) sugar

125 g (4½ oz) unsalted butter, chopped

2 teaspoons apple cider vinegar mixed with 80 ml (2½ fl oz/⅓ cup) cold water and 4 ice cubes

For the pastry, combine the flour, sugar and salt in a bowl. Add the butter pieces and toss to coat. Turn out onto a clean work surface and, using a pastry cutter (or flat-bladed knife), roughly cut the butter into the flour mixture (leave some large chunks of butter as this will help the pastry to become nice and flaky as it cooks).

Create a well in the centre of the flour mixture and add the vinegar water in 3 batches, working it in with your hands to form a rough dough (you may not need all of the water). Shape into a rough disc and wrap in plastic wrap. Chill for 3 hours.

Roll out the pastry on a lightly floured work surface to a circle with a thickness of 3 mm (⅛ in). Line a 22 cm (8¾ in) cast-iron ovenproof frying pan or pie dish with the pastry. Chill for 1 hour.

Meanwhile, make the pie filling. Melt 50 g (1¾ oz) of the butter in a large deep saucepan over medium heat. Add the apples, sugar, golden syrup, cardamom and allspice and cook, stirring, for 15 minutes or until the apples are tender. Remove from the heat and stir through the cream and vanilla, then leave to cool completely.

Melt the remaining butter and combine with half the breadcrumbs and the pecans in a bowl with the salt, using your hands to make sure the breadcrumbs are completely coated in the mixture. Stir the remaining breadcrumbs through the apple mixture.

Preheat the oven to 180°C (350°F). Pour the apple mixture into the pastry case and top with the nutty bread mixture. Bake for 45 minutes or until the pastry and breadcrumbs are a dark golden colour. Remove from the oven and rest for 30 minutes before serving with ice cream.

Blackberry and ginger pie

I spent a glorious afternoon in Glastonbury in the UK with my oldest childhood friend, Khira, looking after her young cousins and picking blackberries from brambles for a pie. I've never tasted blackberries so sweet and ripe, and it was so much fun seeing the girls with stained lips and hands, their faces flushed with excitement as they ate more and more. – *Phoebe*

Serves 6

500 g (1 lb 2 oz) frozen blackberries

110 g (4 oz) caster (superfine) sugar

160 g (5½ oz/½ cup) cherry or raspberry jam

25 g (1 oz) crystallised (candied) ginger, chopped

2 teaspoons cornflour (cornstarch)

1 egg, lightly beaten with 1 tablespoon water

1 tablespoon demerara sugar

thickened (whipping) cream to serve

Pastry

200 g (7 oz/1⅓ cups) plain (all-purpose) flour

55 g (2 oz/¼ cup) caster (superfine) sugar

¼ teaspoon fine sea salt

125 g (4½ oz) cold unsalted butter, cut into 2 cm (¾ in) cubes

2 teaspoons apple cider vinegar mixed with 80 ml (2½ fl oz/⅓ cup) cold water and 4 ice cubes

For the pastry, combine the flour, sugar and salt in a bowl. Add the butter pieces and toss to coat. Turn out onto a clean work surface and, using a pastry cutter (or flat-bladed knife), roughly cut the butter into the flour mixture (leaving some large chunks of butter so the pastry will become nice and flaky). Create a well in the centre of the flour mixture and add the vinegar water in 3 batches, working it in with your hands to form a rough dough (you may not need all the water). Shape into a disc, wrap in plastic wrap and chill for 3 hours.

Roll out one-third of the pastry on a lightly floured work surface to form a 20 cm × 15 cm (8 in × 6 in) rectangle, 3 mm (⅛ in) thick. Cut into fifteen 8 mm × 20 cm (½ in × 8 in) strips. Place them on a baking tray and cover with plastic wrap. Roll out the rest of the pastry to a thickness of 3 mm (⅛ in) and line the base and side of a 17 cm × 3 cm deep (6¾ in × 1¼ in) pie dish. Chill all the pastry for 30 minutes.

Cook the blackberries, sugar, jam and ginger in a saucepan over medium heat for 15 minutes or until syrupy. Mix 3 tablespoons of the syrup with the cornflour until smooth. Return to the saucepan and cook for a further 4 minutes or until thickened. Remove from the heat and leave to cool completely.

Pour the filling into the pastry-lined tin. Make a lattice top with the cooled strips (see page 150) and place it over the filling. Press the edges to seal and trim any excess pastry. Freeze for 1 hour.

Preheat the oven to 200°C (400°F). Brush the pastry with the egg wash and scatter with demerara sugar. Place on a baking tray and bake for 30 minutes or until light golden. Reduce the oven temperature to 180°C (350°F) and cook for 30 minutes or until golden and bubbling. Rest for 30 minutes.

Note If you can't find a 17 cm pie dish, make another half quantity of pastry and bake the pie in a 22 cm pie dish.

Pumpkin pie with candied pepitas

My current obsession is adding vegetables to desserts. I love the earthy flavour and interesting textures that vegetables give to cakes, tarts, ice creams and, of course, pies. However, pumpkin reigns in this classic pie for its delicate, sweet flavour. It marries perfectly with the fragrant spices while being balanced by a punchy sour cream topping. – *Phoebe*

Serves 6

600 g (1 lb 5 oz) peeled butternut pumpkin (squash), chopped into 2 cm ($^3/_4$ in) pieces

375 g (13 oz/1$^1/_2$ cups) sour cream

3 eggs

150 g (5$^1/_2$ oz) demerara sugar

100 g (3$^1/_2$ oz) caster (superfine) sugar

2 teaspoons natural vanilla extract

1$^1/_2$ teaspoons ground ginger

$^1/_2$ teaspoon ground allspice

$^1/_2$ teaspoon ground turmeric

$^1/_4$ teaspoon ground nutmeg

2 tablespoons pepitas (pumpkin seeds)

1 tablespoon maple syrup

125 ml (4 fl oz/$^1/_2$ cup) thickened (whipping) cream

Pastry

200 g (7 oz/1$^1/_3$ cups) plain (all-purpose) flour

55 g (2 oz/$^1/_4$ cup) caster (superfine) sugar

$^1/_4$ teaspoon fine sea salt

125 g (4$^1/_2$ oz) cold unsalted butter, cut into 2 cm ($^3/_4$ in) cubes

2 teaspoons apple cider vinegar mixed with 80 ml (2$^1/_2$ fl oz/$^1/_3$ cup) cold water and 4 ice cubes

For the pastry, combine the flour, sugar and salt in a bowl. Add the butter pieces and toss to coat. Turn out onto a clean work surface and, using a pastry cutter (or flat-bladed knife), roughly cut the butter into the flour (leave some large chunks of butter in the mixture, as this will ensure the pastry becomes nice and flaky as it cooks).

Make a well in the centre of the flour mixture and add the vinegar water in 3 batches, using your hands to fold it into the flour to combine. Shape into a disc, wrap in plastic wrap and chill for 3 hours.

Roll out the pastry on a lightly floured work surface to a thickness of 3 mm ($^1/_8$ in). Use the pastry to line the base and sides of a 15 cm × 8 cm deep (6 in × 3$^1/_4$ in) fluted pie dish. Chill for 1 hour.

Preheat the oven to 200°C (400°F). Line the pastry case with baking paper and fill with baking beads (or uncooked rice or dried beans). Bake for 20 minutes or until the pastry is a light golden colour. Remove the paper and baking weights, and cook for a further 5 minutes or until the pastry base is dry to the touch. Set aside to cool slightly. Reduce the oven temperature to 140°C (275°F).

Steam the pumpkin over a saucepan of simmering water for about 20 minutes or place the pumpkin in a microwave-safe bowl, cover with plastic wrap and microwave on high for 9 minutes, until very tender. Drain in a colander to remove any excess liquid, then leave to cool completely. When cool, whiz in a food processor to a smooth purée. Add 250 g (9 oz/ 1 cup) of the sour cream, the eggs, sugars, vanilla and spices and whiz until smooth and combined. Pour into the pastry case, and bake for 1 hour or until the edge is set but there is a gentle wobble in the centre. Cool to room temperature.

Heat the pepitas and maple syrup in a saucepan over medium heat, stirring, for 1–2 minutes until lightly caramelised. Remove from the heat and leave to cool.

Whisk the remaining sour cream and the cream together until thickened. Serve the pie with the candied pepitas scattered on top, and the sour cream mixture.

Berry, ginger and sour cream pie

Ginger is for me what lavender is for Kirsten (see page 14); I just want to put it in everything! It is so good in pies as it intensifies as it cooks, and cuts through some of the sweetness. – Phoebe

Serves 8

700 g (1 lb 9 oz) frozen mixed berries, e.g. cranberries, raspberries and blueberries

200 g (7 oz) caster (superfine) sugar, plus 2 tablespoons extra

50 g (1¾ oz) roughly chopped crystallised (candied) ginger

2 teaspoons finely grated fresh ginger

1 tablespoon cornflour (cornstarch)

250 g (9 oz) sour cream

1 tablespoon plain (all-purpose) flour

2 eggs

Pastry

375 g (13 oz/2½ cups) plain (all-purpose) flour

55 g (2 oz/¼ cup) caster (superfine) sugar

½ teaspoon fine sea salt

250 g (9 oz) cold unsalted butter, cut into 2 cm (¾ in) pieces

2 tablespoons apple cider vinegar mixed with 125 ml (4 fl oz/½ cup) cold water and 4 ice cubes

For the pastry, combine the flour, sugar and salt in a bowl. Add the butter pieces and toss to coat. Turn out onto a clean work surface and, using a pastry cutter (or flat-bladed knife), roughly cut the butter into the flour mixture (leaving some large chunks of butter so the pastry will become nice and flaky).

Create a well in the centre of the flour mixture and add the vinegar water in 3 batches, working it in with your hands to form a rough dough (you may not need all of the water). Divide the dough in half, shape each piece into a rough disc and wrap in plastic wrap. Chill for 3 hours.

Roll out both pieces of pastry to a thickness of 3 mm (⅛ in). Use one piece to line the base and side of a 22 cm × 3 cm deep (8¾ in × 1¼ in) pie dish. Place the other piece on a baking tray lined with baking paper. Cut a cross in the centre to let steam to escape during cooking. Chill both for 30 minutes.

Preheat the oven to 180°C (350°F). Cook the berries, sugar and both gingers in a saucepan over medium–high heat, stirring occasionally, for 10 minutes or until thick and jammy. Remove from the heat and mix 4 tablespoons of the syrup with the cornflour until smooth. Mix the thickened cornflour into the rest of the syrup in the pan and cook for 1 minute or until combined. Leave to cool completely.

Whisk together the sour cream, flour, 1 tablespoon of the extra caster sugar and 1 egg until combined.

Spoon the berry mixture into the pastry-lined pie dish and pour the sour cream mixture over the top. Cover with the pastry sheet. Whisk the remaining egg with 1 tablespoon of water and brush over the pastry, then scatter with the remaining 1 tablespoon of caster sugar. Bake on a baking tray for 50 minutes or until golden and bubbling. Cool for 30 minutes.

Sweet potato and maple pie

Pumpkin pie is delicious, I don't deny it, but personally I'm a sweet potato fan. The addition of the white chocolate to this recipe gives the pie an amazing fudgy texture, and the maple syrup and brown sugar taste like a beautiful light caramel. Push your boundaries and don't be afraid to put vegetables in your desserts! – *Phoebe*

Serves 8

800 g (1 lb 12 oz) sweet potato, peeled and chopped into 2 cm (¾ in) pieces

50 g (1¾ oz) cold unsalted butter, chopped

1 vanilla bean, split lengthways and seeds scraped

100 g (3½ oz) white chocolate, finely chopped

2 eggs

125 ml (4 fl oz/½ cup) maple syrup, plus extra to serve

60 g (2 oz) soft brown sugar

125 g (4½ oz/½ cup) sour cream

½ teaspoon ground ginger

Base

350 g (12½ oz) ginger nut biscuits (ginger snaps)

80 g (2¾ oz) unsalted butter, melted then cooled

For the base, whiz the biscuits in a food processor to fine crumbs. Pulse in the butter, then press the mixture into the base and side of a 20 cm × 3 cm (8 in × 1¼ in) loose-based cake tin. Chill until needed.

Preheat the oven to 200°C (400°F) and line a baking tray with baking paper. Toss together the sweet potato, butter and vanilla pod and seeds on the tray, making sure they are in a single layer, and roast for 1 hour or until very tender and lightly caramelised. Reduce the oven temperature to 160°C (320°F).

Transfer the cooked potato (discarding the vanilla pod) to a food processor and process until smooth. With the motor running, add the white chocolate until melted and combined, then, with the motor still running, add the eggs, maple syrup, brown sugar, sour cream and ground ginger to form a smooth purée.

Spread the sweet potato mixture over the chilled base and bake for 45 minutes or until set. Cool to room temperature, then chill for 2 hours or until firm. Remove from the tin and cut into thick slices to serve.

Note Instead of sweet potato, I've swapped in roasted carrots and it's just as moreish.

Rhubarb, orange and pistachio pie

My partner, Simon, fancies himself a bit of a rhubarb connoisseur. His family home in New Zealand has the most incredible kitchen garden which is constantly overflowing with whatever is in season. In the spring, there is rhubarb. There's always pressure when it comes to him trying one of my rhubarb desserts but he ate his whole piece of this pie in silence and then went back for more. So it must be good, then. – *Phoebe*

Serves 8

700 g (1 lb 9 oz) rhubarb, trimmed and cut into 10 cm (4 in) pieces

220 g (8 oz) caster (superfine) sugar

juice and finely grated zest of 1 orange

1 egg, lightly beaten with 1 tablespoon water

1 tablespoon demerara sugar

slivered pistachios to serve

Pastry

375 g (13 oz/2½ cups) plain (all-purpose) flour

55 g (2 oz/¼ cup) caster (superfine) sugar

½ teaspoon fine sea salt

250 g (9 oz) cold unsalted butter, cut into 2 cm (¾ in) cubes

2 tablespoons apple cider vinegar mixed with 125 ml (4 fl oz /½ cup) cold water and 4 ice cubes

Frangipane

110 g (4 oz) unsalted butter, softened

110 g (4 oz) caster (superfine) sugar

60 g (2 oz/¼ cup) sour cream

1 egg, plus 1 egg yolk

1 teaspoon natural vanilla extract

250 g (9 oz/1⅔ cups) pistachio nuts, finely ground

50 g (1¾ oz/⅓ cup) plain (all-purpose) flour

To make the pastry, combine the flour, sugar and salt in a bowl. Add the butter pieces and toss to coat. Turn out onto a clean work surface and, using a pastry cutter (or flat-bladed knife), roughly cut the butter into the flour (leave some large chunks of butter as this will help the pastry to become nice and flaky as it cooks).

Create a well in the centre of the flour mixture and add the vinegar water in 3 batches, working it in with your hands to form a rough dough (you may not need all of the water). Divide the dough in half, shape into rough discs and wrap in plastic wrap. Chill for 3 hours.

Roll out one piece of pastry to a thickness of 3 mm (⅛ in). Use the pastry to line the base and sides of a 28 cm × 17 cm (11 in × 6¾ in) pie dish, leaving a 3 cm (1¼ in) overhang. Roll out the second piece of pastry to a thickness of 3 mm (⅛ in) and cut into seven 5 cm (2 in) thick strips. Chill both for 30 minutes.

Combine the rhubarb, caster sugar and orange zest and juice in a saucepan over medium heat. Cook, stirring occasionally, for 15 minutes or until the rhubarb is soft. Remove from the heat and leave to cool completely.

Preheat the oven to 200°C (400°F). For the frangipane, beat the butter and sugar until pale using an electric mixer. Beat in the sour cream, egg and egg yolk, and the vanilla until combined, then beat in the pistachios and flour. Spread into the base of the prepared pie dish and top with the rhubarb mixture.

Make a lattice top with the chilled strips and place it on top of the filling. Trim off any excess pastry from the strips then fold over the overhanging pastry to conceal the ends of the lattice and to seal. Brush with the egg wash and scatter with demerara sugar.

Place on a baking tray and bake for 50 minutes or until golden and bubbling. Rest for 30 minutes, then scatter with the slivered pistachios before serving.

Nectarine, brown butter and honey pie

Nectarines are my favourite fruit but the season just isn't long enough. It felt a little criminal cooking these beautiful summer nectarines into a pie but the result was so good I absolved myself of guilt. Brown butter is the dessert ingredient of the moment: nutty, fatty and rich, it goes so well with pies, crumbles, creamy desserts and cake frostings. I only put a little sweetener in this pie as I rely on the fruit being sweet and in season, but add more or less depending on the time of year and your own palate. – *Phoebe*

Serves 8

70 g (2½ oz) unsalted butter

500 g (1 lb 2 oz) nectarines (about 3), stones removed and chopped

1 teaspoon vanilla bean paste

115 g (4 oz/⅓ cup) honey

1 teaspoon plain (all-purpose) flour

2 sheets frozen butter puff pastry (total 330 g/ 11½ oz), thawed, and if needed, rolled to a thickness of 2 mm (⅛ in)

1 egg, lightly beaten

1 tablespoon demerara sugar

Melt the butter in a large deep saucepan over medium–high heat for 4–5 minutes until a nutty brown. Pour the butter into a small bowl and set aside. Reduce the heat to medium–low. Add the nectarines, vanilla and honey and cook, stirring occasionally, for 30 minutes or until the nectarines are softened and jammy. Remove from the heat.

Preheat the oven to 200°C (400°F). Cut the sheets of pastry in half and then press the ends of two of them together, overlapping by about 3 cm (1¼ in), to form a 36 cm × 15 cm (14½ in × 6 in) rectangle. Place on a baking tray lined with baking paper.

Press the remaining two pieces together to form another 36 cm × 15 cm (14½ in × 6 in) rectangle. Using a serrated knife, shallowly score the pastry about 8 mm (⅓ in) apart, leaving a 1 cm (½ in) border the whole way around.

Spread the nectarine mixture over the first rectangle, leaving a 2 cm (¾ in) border all the way around the edge. Brush the edges with the beaten egg. Cover with the second rectangle and press the edges to seal, then brush with the egg and scatter with the demerara sugar. Bake for 30 minutes or until bubbling and golden. Leave to cool for 30 minutes before slicing.

Nutella pie

This pie reminds me of the first time I ever tried a molten Nutella crepe, standing on the roadside on the Rue Mouffetard in Paris. It was my first trip overseas, and Paris was the first stop. I remember feeling so impossibly uncouth as warm Nutella dripped all over my hands. I demolished one crepe and then ordered another. The addition of Nutella gives this custard a decadent, fudgy texture. – Phoebe

Serves 12

400 g (14 oz) Nutella

3 eggs, plus 2 egg yolks

400 ml (13½ fl oz) pouring (single/light) cream

1 tablespoon plain (all-purpose) flour

30 g (1 oz) roasted hazelnuts, some left whole and some roughly crushed, to serve

Pastry

200 g (7 oz/1⅓ cups) plain (all-purpose) flour

¼ teaspoon fine sea salt

55 g (2 oz/¼ cup) caster (superfine) sugar

125 g (4½ oz) cold unsalted butter, cut into 2 cm (¾ in) cubes

2 teaspoons apple cider vinegar mixed with 80 ml (2½ fl oz/⅓ cup) cold water and 4 ice cubes

For the pastry, combine the flour, sugar and salt in a bowl. Add the butter pieces and toss to coat. Turn out onto a clean work surface and, using a pastry cutter (or flat-bladed knife), roughly cut the butter into the flour mixture (leave some large chunks of butter as this will help the pastry to become nice and flaky as it cooks).

Create a well in the centre of the flour mixture and add the vinegar water in 3 batches, working it in with your hands to form a rough dough (you may not need all of the water). Shape into a rough disc and wrap in plastic wrap. Chill for 3 hours.

Roll out the pastry on a lightly floured work surface to a thickness of 3 mm (⅛ in) thick. Use the pastry to line the base and side of a 22 cm (8¾ in) pie dish leaving 3 cm (1¼ in) overhang. Using your thumb and index finger, pinch the overhang to form a fluted edge. Freeze for 30 minutes.

Preheat the oven to 200°C (400°F). Line the pastry case with baking paper and fill with baking beads (or uncooked rice or dried beans). Bake for 25 minutes or until the pastry is a light golden colour. Remove the paper and baking beads, and bake for a further 5 minutes or until the base is just dry. Remove from the oven and leave to cool. Reduce the oven temperature to 140°C (275°F).

For the filling, whisk together the Nutella, eggs and egg yolks, and the cream in a bowl until smooth. Whisk the flour with 3 tablespoons of the Nutella mixture until smooth, then stir into the rest of the mixture to combine. Strain into the cooled pastry case and bake for 1 hour or until the edge is set but there is still a gentle wobble in the centre. Cool to room temperature, then serve.

Mixed berry pie

This is my go-to pie recipe. Whenever I have loads of berries in the freezer I'll make this pie and add pears or apples to the filling. It's beautiful and jammy and I love standing at the stove stirring the fruit, it's so therapeutic. Make this pie on a lazy Sunday, and enjoy it! – *Phoebe*

Serves 6

500 g (1 lb 2 oz) mixed frozen berries, e.g. blueberries, raspberries and cranberries

2 ripe pears, peeled, cored and chopped

220 g (8 oz) caster (superfine) sugar

1 teaspoon natural vanilla extract

35 g (1¼ oz) vanilla custard powder

1 egg, lightly beaten

1 tablespoon demerara sugar

Pastry

375 g (13 oz/2½ cups) plain (all-purpose) flour

55 g (2 oz/¼ cup) caster (superfine) sugar

½ teaspoon fine sea salt

250 g (9 oz) cold unsalted butter, cut into 2 cm (¾ in) pieces

2 tablespoons apple cider vinegar mixed with 125 ml (4 fl oz/½ cup) cold water and 4 ice cubes

To make the pastry, combine the flour, sugar and salt in a bowl. Add the butter pieces and toss to coat. Turn out onto a clean work surface and, using a pastry cutter (or flat-bladed knife), roughly cut the butter into the flour (leave some large chunks of butter in the mixture as this will help the pastry to become nice and flaky as it cooks).

Create a well in the centre of the flour mixture and add the vinegar water in 3 batches, working it in with your hands to form a rough dough (you may not need all of the water). Divide the dough in half, shape into rough discs and wrap in plastic wrap. Chill for 3 hours.

Working with one piece of pastry at a time, roll out on a lightly floured work surface to a thickness of 3 mm (⅛ in) thick. Use the first pastry sheet to line the base and side of a 22 cm (8¾ in) pie dish, leaving a 3 cm (1¼ in) overhang. Roll out the second piece of pastry to a thickness of 3 mm (⅛ in) and cut into eight 3 cm (1¼ in) wide strips. Chill both for 1 hour.

Bring the berries, pears and sugar to a simmer in a saucepan over medium heat. Cook for 15 minutes or until syrupy. Remove from the heat and stir in the vanilla, then mix 4 tablespoons of the berry mixture with the custard powder until smooth. Return to the pan with the rest of the syrup and cook for 5 minutes, stirring, or until thickened. Remove from the heat and leave to cool completely.

Preheat the oven to 200°C (400°F). Place the lined pie dish on a baking tray and fill with the berry mixture. Make a lattice top with the chilled strips (see page 150), place it over the filling and press to seal. Trim off any excess pastry, then fold over the overhanging pastry to conceal the ends of the lattice strips and to seal. Using your thumb and forefinger, press to form a fluted edge. Brush with the beaten egg, scatter with demerara sugar and bake for 20 minutes or until the pastry is turning a golden colour. Reduce the temperature to 180°C (350°F) and cook for a further 30 minutes or until the pastry is crisp and golden, and the filling is bubbling. Rest for 30 minutes before serving.

cheats

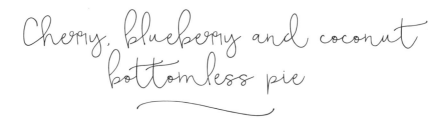

Cherry, blueberry and coconut bottomless pie

There are sometimes those recipes that come along that you just really love. You love the way they look, you love the way they taste and you love the way others respond to them. This is one of them. It is so easy to make, tastes brilliant, is beautifully oozy and has the nostalgia of a good crumble. Yes, it has no pie base but that just means it's all about the fruit and topping (and that's why we call it a cheats' pie). Hope you love it as much as we do. – Kirsten

Serves 4

720 g (1 lb 9 oz) pitted morello cherries, drained, juice reserved (about 350 ml/12 fl oz)

180 g (6½ oz) caster (superfine) sugar

2 tablespoons cornflour (cornstarch)

100 g (3½ oz) frozen blueberries

Streusel topping

75 g (2¾ oz) cold unsalted butter, chopped

1½ tablespoons soft brown sugar

35 g (1¼ oz) desiccated (dried shredded) coconut

35 g (1¼ oz/¼ cup) plain (all-purpose) flour

90 g (3 oz) rolled (porridge) oats

2 tablespoons slivered almonds

cream or ice cream to serve

Bring the cherry juice and sugar to a rapid simmer in a saucepan over medium–high heat for 15 minutes, stirring to dissolve the sugar, or until reduced by half. Combine 4 tablespoons of the cherry syrup with the cornflour in a small bowl, then stir the thickened cornflour into the rest of the syrup in the saucepan, along with the cherries and blueberries. Simmer for a further 10 minutes or until the liquid is thick and glossy. Remove from the heat and leave to cool completely. Preheat the oven to 180°C (350°F).

For the streusel topping, combine all the ingredients in a bowl, rubbing the butter into the dry ingredients but leaving some big chunks of butter.

Pour the pie filling into a shallow baking dish and scatter over the crumbly topping. Place on a baking tray and bake for 35 minutes or until bubbling and jammy. Serve with cream or ice cream.

Plum, almond and orange blossom crostata with sugared thyme

When we showed my family the first round of photographs from this book, they all pointed to this as their favourite. I think it's partly because it looks so accessible and easy, which it is. No rolling of pastry, and frangipane is so simple to master. I'm super-fussy when it comes to stone fruit, as my parents grew the most amazing fruit on their orchard when I was a kid. Plums remind me of our big old dehydrator whirring through the night, and waking up in the morning to beautiful sweet and sour semi-dried plums. While everyone else was having roll-ups at school, that's what my sisters and I were eating! – *Phoebe*

Serves 12

435 g (15½ oz) frozen Careme vanilla bean pastry, thawed, or other bought sweet shortcrust rolled to a thickness of 3 mm (⅛ in)

180 g (6½ oz) unsalted butter, at room temperature

240 g (8½ oz) caster (superfine) sugar

finely grated zest of 2 oranges, plus pared zest of 1 orange

1 tablespoon orange blossom water

2 teaspoons vanilla bean paste

3 eggs, plus 1 egg white

300 g (10½ oz/3 cups) almond meal

2 tablespoons cornflour (cornstarch)

1 kg (2 lb 3 oz) ripe plums, halved and stones removed

1 tablespoon demerara sugar

6 thyme sprigs

icing (confectioners') sugar, to dust (optional)

Preheat the oven to 180°C (350°F). Line a baking tray with baking paper and lay the pastry on top. Chill until needed.

Using an electric mixer, beat the butter and caster sugar until pale, reserving 1 tablespoon of the sugar. Beat in the orange zest, orange blossom water and vanilla, then the whole eggs, one at a time, beating well after each addition. Finally, beat in the almond meal and cornflour to combine.

Spread the frangipane mixture over the pastry, leaving a 1 cm (½ in) border all the way round. Fold in the edges to partially enclose. Top with the plums, and scatter with the demerara sugar and the pared orange zest.

Lightly whisk the egg white and dip the thyme sprigs into it, then coat them in the reserved tablespoon of caster sugar. Scatter over the crostata and bake for 35 minutes or until the pastry is golden and the plums are soft. Once cool, dust with icing sugar, if desired.

Caramel apple pie

In the picture, this pie is housed in a family heirloom: a cast-iron frying pan that we've had since I was born. When I was seven my parents took my sisters and me on an amazing six-month trip around Australia in a caravan. This pan was the vessel for months of Dad's bolognese, sausages, baked beans and freshly caught fish, quite possibly pancakes (if we were lucky) but never pie. Nostalgia can be attached to the strangest things but I've always loved the fact that this pan lives permanently in our family kitchen and I jumped at the opportunity to put it in the book. This caramel apple pie is such a cinch to make with a good pan and a good piece of bought pastry. – *Phoebe*

Serves 8

850 g (1 lb 14 oz) sharp green apples, e.g. Granny Smith apples, peeled, cored and chopped

450 g (1 lb) jar dulce de leche

1 teaspoon ground cinnamon

60 ml (2 fl oz/¼ cup) pouring (single/light) cream

2 × 435 g (15½ oz) frozen Careme vanilla bean pastry, thawed, or other bought sweet shortcrust rolled to a thickness of 3 mm (⅛ in)

35 g (1¼ oz) vanilla custard powder

1 egg, lightly beaten

1 tablespoon demerara sugar

You can make your own dulce de leche by boiling two 395 g (14 oz) tins of sweetened condensed milk, if you prefer. Remove and discard the labels from the tins, then make two holes in the lid of each using a tin opener. Place the tins in a saucepan, open side up, and fill the saucepan with cold water to about 1 cm (½ in) below the tops of the tins. Bring to the boil over high heat, then reduce the heat to medium–low and simmer for 3 hours. Keep topping up the water. Carefully remove the tins and leave to cool, then open the tins and scoop out the caramel. You may have a bit left over after making this recipe but that's no bad thing!

Preheat the oven to 200°C (400°F). Cook the apples, dulce de leche and cinnamon in a large saucepan over medium–high heat, stirring often, for 10 minutes or until the apples are slightly softened. Remove from the heat and leave to cool completely. Stir through the cream.

Line a 26 cm (10¼ in) ovenproof frying pan or pie dish with half of the pastry. Scatter the custard powder over the top then spoon in the apple mixture. Top with the remaining pastry, trim any excess from the top layer that doesn't match up with the bottom and press to seal. Cut a cross in the top of the pastry using a sharp knife. Brush the pastry with the beaten egg then scatter with the demerara sugar. Bake for 40 minutes or until the pastry is golden. Rest for 30 minutes before serving.

Apple and strawberry jam pie

We photographed this pie outside on my parents' concrete deck in the Blue Mountains, smack bang in the middle of a freezing winter. Nothing was more satisfying than finishing the shot and heading inside for a big spoonful of hot, jammy fruit and pastry. I love putting big chunks of white chocolate in pies as they create a delicious fudgy surprise when you come across them. This pie has no base, so is super-fast to make and perfect to whip up midweek. – *Phoebe*

Serves 6

435 g (15½ oz) frozen Careme vanilla bean pastry, thawed, or other bought sweet shortcrust rolled to a thickness of 3 mm (⅛ in)

600 g (1 lb 5 oz) apples, peeled, cored and sliced

1 vanilla bean, split lengthways and seeds scraped

75 g (2¾ oz) caster (superfine) sugar

80 g (2¾ oz/⅓ cup) soft brown sugar

40 g (1½ oz) unsalted butter

320 g (11½ oz) strawberry jam

125 g (4½ oz) strawberries, hulled

2 teaspoons cornflour (cornstarch)

100 g (4 oz) white chocolate, chopped

1 egg, lightly beaten

demerara sugar, for sprinkling

Preheat the oven to 180°C (350°F). Place the apples in a large frying pan with the vanilla pod and seeds, caster sugar, brown sugar and butter, and cook, stirring, for 25 minutes or until softened. Stir through the strawberry jam, strawberries and cornflour and set aside to cool.

Place a 30 cm × 20 cm (12 in × 8 in) pie dish on a baking tray. Fold the white chocolate into the filling mixture, then pour into the dish. Cut five 4 cm (1½ in) wide strips of pastry and seven 1 cm (½ in) wide strips and lay over the filling, alternating the size of the strips, to form a lattice top. Trim off any excess pastry and brush with the beaten egg and sprinkle with demerara sugar. Bake for 35 minutes or until golden and bubbling. Cool to room temperature, then serve.

Baked raspberry jam custard pie

This one is for my grandpa. In my early twenties I travelled through Europe for six months and was lucky enough to base myself in England with Grandpa Noo Noo. We were known as the odd couple: we bickered like a married couple and had a hilarious time together. We would drive out to the countryside on the weekends to explore beautiful old pubs and eat traditional English pub food. Noo Noo never seemed as excited about the main menu as he did the desserts, and often earmarked the dessert he would have before deciding on his main. On my first day at his house, I opened the small fridge in the kitchen and saw shelf after shelf filled with sweet pastries, doughnuts, glazed fruit tarts, big blocks of chocolate and anything with jam in it! Nothing on the shelves was of a savoury nature – although after closer inspection of the vegetable crisper, I found an exhausted looking piece of broccoli. When I asked Noo Noo why there was only broccoli and nothing else in the fridge to go with it, he answered: 'That's there to make me feel better. I probably won't get around to cooking it but I'm definitely healthier for it being there'. Noo Noo, this one's for you. Eat custard and jam pie to your heart's content and I will never dob on you to Mum, it's all yours. Love you. – Kirsten

Serves 8

435 g (15½ oz) frozen Careme vanilla bean pastry, thawed, or other bought sweet shortcrust rolled to a thickness of 3 mm (⅛ in)

2 tablespoons vanilla custard powder

1 tablespoon caster (superfine) sugar

1 teaspoon natural vanilla extract

500 ml (17 fl oz/2 cups) pouring (single/light) cream

160 g (5½ oz/½ cup) good-quality raspberry jam

Line a 22 cm (8¾ in) pie dish with the pastry and trim the edges, leaving a 3 cm (1¼ in) overhang. Using your thumb and index finger, pinch the overhang of the pastry to form a fluted edge. Freeze for 1 hour.

Whisk together the custard powder, sugar and vanilla in a bowl. Add 2 tablespoons of the cream and whisk until smooth. Transfer to a saucepan over medium heat and add the remaining cream. Cook, stirring constantly, for 6 minutes or until thick and smooth. Remove from the heat and cool completely to room temperature.

Preheat the oven to 200°C (400°F). Line the pastry case with baking paper and fill with baking beads (or uncooked rice or dried beans). Place the pie dish on a large baking tray and cook for 10 minutes or until just dry, then remove the baking beads and paper, and bake for 10 minutes or until the pastry is golden. Cool slightly then spread the jam over the base of the pastry and top with the custard. Place in the oven and immediately reduce the temperature to 150°C (300°F). Bake for 40 minutes or until the custard is set but still has a wobble in the centre. Cool completely, then chill until cold.

Apple and sour cream crostata

I love the creamy acidic addition of sour cream in desserts. Here, it softens the usually very sweet frangipane and crisp, sharp apples. This pie is fast and easy to make, with little technique required. You could easily add other seasonal fruits like plums, rhubarb, blackberries or strawberries to this crostata to make it extra special. – Phoebe

Serves 8

445 g (15½ oz) frozen Careme sour cream pastry, thawed, or 1 × portion of pastry from the Spiced apple and golden syrup pie (see page 28)

110 g (4 oz) unsalted butter, softened

110 g (4 oz) caster (superfine) sugar

60 g (2 oz/¼ cup) sour cream

1 teaspoon vanilla bean paste

2 eggs, plus 1 egg yolk

250 g (9 oz) almond meal

2 sharp green apples, e.g. Granny Smith apples, peeled, cored and thinly sliced into rounds

2 tablespoons demerara sugar

icing (confectioners') sugar to dust

cream to serve

Preheat the oven to 180°C (350°F). Line a 22 cm (8¾ in) pie dish with the pastry, leaving a 5 cm (2 in) overhang. Chill in the fridge while you make the frangipane.

For the frangipane, beat the butter and caster sugar using an electric mixer until pale. Beat in the sour cream and vanilla bean paste, then add the eggs and egg yolks one at a time, beating well after each addition. Fold through the almond meal.

Spread the frangipane over the pastry and arrange the apple slices over the top. Scatter with the demerara sugar and bake for 40 minutes or until golden and just set. Cool to room temperature, dust with icing sugar and serve with cream.

Note This pie would also be delicious with the pie crust from the Spiced apple and golden syrup pie (see page 28), so if you have time, you can make this a proper homemade pie.

Banana and whisky pie

Boozy caramel fruit, flaky pastry and creamy smooth filling: this is such an easy dessert. It takes a couple of separate elements and brings them effortlessly together to produce a great result. Feel free to cut the bananas anyway you like, and substitute pineapple slices for the banana for another tropical version. – Kirsten

Serves 6

2 sheets frozen butter puff pastry (total weight 330 g/11½ oz), thawed, and if needed, rolled to a thickness of 2 mm (⅛ in)

500 g (1 lb 2 oz) cream cheese, at room temperature

2 teaspoons vanilla bean paste

180 g (6½ oz) caster (superfine) sugar

2 tablespoons whisky

3 bananas, peeled and halved lengthways

3 tablespoons chopped roasted hazelnuts to serve

Preheat the oven to 200°C (400°F). Place the puff pastry sheets on top of each other in a 20 cm (8 in) pie dish and trim the edges leaving a 2 cm (¾ in) overhang. Line the pastry with baking paper and fill with baking beads (or uncooked rice or dried beans) and bake for 25 minutes or until the edges are puffed and golden. Remove the paper and baking beads. Using a fork, prick the base to release any air, then bake for a further 5 minutes or until the base is golden and dry to the touch. Remove from the oven and leave to cool completely.

Mix the cream cheese, vanilla and 40 g (1½ oz) of the sugar in a food processor until smooth.

Heat the remaining sugar with 2 tablespoons of water in a frying pan over medium–high heat for 5 minutes, swirling the pan occasionally, or until it forms a golden caramel. Tipping the pan away from you, add the whisky, swirling to combine. Carefully add the bananas, cut side down, and cook for 3 minutes until they are a dark golden colour. Turn over the bananas and remove from the heat.

Spread the cream cheese mixture over the pastry base, then top with the bananas, extra caramel from the pan and the hazelnuts.

Apricot, strawberry and vanilla pie

Apricot jam always reminds me of culinary school. We used it to glaze everything we made in patisserie, from pastry swans to basic scones. I thought it was daggy then, but now, when I mix it with a little vanilla and bake it in a pie, it tastes really good, and even better with strawberries. You could use raspberries or fresh pitted cherries in this pie too. – Phoebe

Serves 6

3 sheets frozen butter puff pastry (total 500 g/ 1 lb 2 oz), thawed, and if needed, rolled to a thickness of 2 mm ($\frac{1}{8}$ in)

750 g (1 lb 11 oz) strawberries, hulled (halve any very large ones)

70 g ($2\frac{1}{2}$ oz) caster (superfine) sugar

350 g ($12\frac{1}{2}$ oz) apricot jam

1 teaspoon vanilla bean paste

juice of 1 lemon

3 tablespoons cornflour (cornstarch)

1 egg, lightly beaten with 1 tablespoon water

1 tablespoon demerara sugar

Line a 20 cm (8 in) pie dish with one sheet of the pastry, trimming to fit. Chill until needed. Cut the remaining sheets into twelve 12 cm × 2 cm ($4\frac{3}{4}$ in × $\frac{3}{4}$ in) strips, discarding any excess pastry. On a baking tray lined with baking paper, weave the pastry strips into a tight lattice pattern (see page 150). Freeze until needed.

Preheat the oven to 200°C (400°F). Line the pastry case with baking paper and fill with baking beads (or uncooked rice or dried beans). Place the pie dish on a large baking tray and cook for 15 minutes or until the pastry is a light golden colour. Remove from the oven, but keep the oven on. Remove the paper and baking beads from the pastry case and prick the base with a fork to release any air, then cook for a further 5 minutes or until it is dry to the touch. Allow to cool to room temperature.

Toss together the strawberries, caster sugar, jam, vanilla, lemon juice and cornflour in a bowl and transfer to the pie dish. Place the lattice on top of the filling. Press the edges to seal and trim around the edge.

Brush the pie with the egg wash, then scatter with the demerara sugar. Bake for 50 minutes or until golden and cooked. Leave to cool for 30 minutes before serving.

Lemon and blueberry meringue pie

There could not be a pie book without a lemon meringue pie! But why make it a long, process-heavy pie when you can get the same result from a much quicker and easier recipe?! This recipe uses store-bought lemon curd, with the addition of fresh blueberries and simple meringue piped on top. The inspiration for this inventive meringue swirl came from a story Phoebe wrote for *delicious.* magazine. We loved the result of that pie and wanted to re-create it for this book. The deep charred marshmallow meringue you see is achieved by using a kitchen blowtorch. If you don't have a blowtorch, put your pie under a piping hot grill (broiler) for 1–2 minutes until nice and caramelised. – *Kirsten*

Serves 6

½ × 435 g (15½ oz) frozen Careme vanilla bean pastry, thawed, or other bought sweet shortcrust rolled to a thickness of 3 mm (⅛ in)

250 g (9 oz) mascarpone cheese

315 g (11 oz/1 cup) lemon curd

125 g (4½ oz) fresh blueberries

3 egg whites

160 g (5½ oz) caster (superfine) sugar

Use the pastry to line a 16 cm (6¼ in) springform cake tin, roughly folding in the edges. Chill for 30 minutes.

Preheat the oven to 200°C (400°F). Line the pastry case with baking paper and fill with baking beads (or uncooked rice or dried beans). Bake for 25 minutes or until the pastry is a light golden colour, then remove the paper and baking beads, and bake for a further 10 minutes or until the base is golden and dry to the touch. Cool completely and carefully remove from the cake tin.

Fold the mascarpone, lemon curd and blueberries together in a bowl. Spread the mixture in the base of the pastry case.

Using an electric mixer, whisk the egg whites and sugar together for 10 minutes until stiff and glossy and the sugar has dissolved. Transfer to a piping (icing) bag fitted with a 1 cm (½ in) nozzle and pipe a spiral of meringue over the filling. Using a kitchen blowtorch, caramelise the meringue and serve immediately.

Quince, berry and bay sugar pie

My parents have a beautiful old quince tree on their farm in Bathurst, New South Wales. It only fruits biannually, so every second year they load me up with a big box of quinces to take home. There are always so many and this year I finally got around to preserving some and keeping them in jars in my kitchen to add to desserts, salads and tagines. In the winter, Mum and I cooked up a big pot of quince paste together. It was so beautiful to watch the hues of the fruit change from crisp white, to a soft orange and then a deep, rich purple as it cooked. We made a few kilos and packaged it up in baking paper and airtight jars as it lasts for ages. This pie is really just an excuse to use up some of that lush thick sugary paste, and the bay is a beautiful contrast with its strong savoury notes. – *Phoebe*

Serves 8

2 × 435 g (15½ oz) frozen Careme vanilla bean pastry, thawed, or other bought sweet shortcrust rolled to a thickness of 3 mm (⅛ in)

250 g (9 oz) strawberries, hulled and chopped

125 g (4½ oz) raspberries

2 tablespoons caster (superfine) sugar

220 g (8 oz/½ cup) quince paste, softened

1 egg, lightly beaten

2 dried bay leaves, crushed

Preheat the oven to 180°C (350°F). Line a baking tray with baking paper and place one of the rolled-out pieces of pastry on it. Trim to 30 cm × 21 cm (12 in × 8¼ in).

Toss the strawberries and raspberries with 1 tablespoon of the sugar in a bowl. Spread the first sheet of pastry with quince paste, leaving a 2 cm (¾ in) border, and scatter the berries over the top of the quince paste.

Cover with the second rolled-out piece of pastry and trim the edges, pressing to seal. Brush with the beaten egg and bake for 40 minutes or until golden and bubbling.

Meanwhile, combine the remaining sugar with the bay leaves in a bowl. Scatter over the pie, then slice and serve.

Roasted strawberries and cream pie

The roasted strawberries in this pie soften to a gorgeous jammy summer berry syrup, which, when paired with a thick vanilla cream is the ultimate flavour combination. I recently discovered a little patch of strawberries in my community garden and can't resist plucking the sweet little berries straight from the plant (yes, I'm the community garden thief). Strawberries and cream are so classically beautiful together, and the thyme gives this recipe a beautiful earthy flavour that I love. – *Phoebe*

Serves 10

435 g (15½ oz) frozen Careme vanilla bean pastry, thawed, or other bought sweet shortcrust rolled to a thickness of 3 mm (⅛ in)

750 g (1 lb 11 oz) strawberries, hulled (halve any very large ones)

1 vanilla bean, split lengthways and seeds scraped

2 tablespoons maple syrup

1 thyme sprig, plus extra to decorate

500 g (1 lb 2 oz) mascarpone cheese

375 ml (12½ fl oz/1½ cups) thickened (whipping) cream

4 tablespoons pure icing (confectioners') sugar

1 teaspoon vanilla bean paste

Preheat the oven to 200°C (400°F). Line the base and side of a 22 cm × 5 cm deep (8¾ in × 2 in) pie dish with the pastry and trim away the excess. Line the pastry case with baking paper and fill with baking beads (or uncooked rice or dried beans). Place on a baking tray and cook for 20 minutes or until golden, then remove the baking beads and paper, and cook for a further 5 minutes or until the base is dry to the touch. Set aside and leave to cool completely. Keep the oven on.

Toss together the strawberries, vanilla pod and seeds, maple syrup and thyme on a baking tray lined with baking paper, and roast for 16 minutes or until softened and slightly syrupy. Cool to room temperature.

Whisk the mascarpone, cream, icing sugar and vanilla bean paste together in a bowl until thick. Spread into the cooled pie crust and top with the roasted strawberries and their syrup.

Salted chocolate and date pie

No baking needed here: just crushed-up biscuits (cookies), blended-up fresh dates and a seriously smooth chocolate ganache. An incredibly easy and straightforward recipe with some real wow! I know we've been hammered with 'salted caramel' recently, but salt added to chocolate is still really underrated. The French have been sprinkling a bit of salt in their chocolate for years. Think of it as the same as seasoning your savoury food, it enhances the other flavours that its hanging out with. — Kirsten

Serves 16
Makes 2 × 16 cm (6¼ in) pies

250 g (9 oz) Medjool dates, pitted

300 g (10½ oz) plain chocolate biscuits (cookies)

100 g (3½ oz) unsalted butter

300 g (10½ oz) dark chocolate, finely chopped

400 ml (13½ fl oz) thickened (whipping) cream

1 teaspoon sea salt flakes

Place the dates in a bowl and cover with 170 ml (5½ fl oz/⅔ cup) of boiling water. Set aside for 30 minutes to soften.

Pulse the biscuits in a food processor to fine crumbs. Pulse in the butter, then press the mixture into the bases and sides of two 16 cm × 4 cm deep (6¼ in × 1½ in) pie dishes and chill while you make the filling.

Drain the dates and place in a food processor with 2 tablespoons of boiling water. Process until very smooth. Spread over the biscuit bases and chill.

Place the chopped chocolate in a heatproof bowl. Heat the cream in a saucepan to just below boiling point, then pour over the chocolate and stir until melted and smooth. Pour over the top of the date purée and smooth the surface, then chill for 1 hour until the chocolate has set. Scatter over the salt flakes to serve.

hand

Brown butter baklava handpies with figs and honey

These pies looked so beautiful when we were preparing them. Uncooked, the pastry is tapered and white, the nuts textural and the plump figs rest like a sculpture in the centre. This recipe is a really perfect end to a Mediterranean feast, and the pies taste great hot or cold with a big dollop of yoghurt. They are the ultimate cheat's version of one of my all-time favourite desserts, baklava. – *Phoebe*

Makes 4

6 sheets fresh filo pastry

50 g (1¾ oz) unsalted butter, melted and cooled

320 g (11½ oz) mixed crushed nuts, e.g. pistachio nuts, hazelnuts and walnuts

2 eggs

110 g (4 oz) caster (superfine) sugar

4 ripe figs, halved

90 g (3 oz/¼ cup) honey, plus extra to serve

honeycomb (optional) to serve

plain Greek-style yoghurt (optional) to serve

Preheat the oven to 180°C (350°F). Working with one sheet of pastry at a time, brush each one liberally with butter, laying the buttered sheets on top of each other. Using a sharp knife, cut the layered pastry into four equal squares. Line four 11 cm (4¼ in) pie dishes with the pastry.

Combine the nuts, eggs and sugar in a bowl, then divide the mixture among each lined pie dish. Place 2 fig halves on top of each, and drizzle with the honey.

Bake for 20 minutes or until the pastry is golden and crisp, and the figs are bursting. Drizzle with extra honey, top with honeycomb (if using) and serve with a dollop of yoghurt (if using).

Fried apricot and cardamom sugar handpies

We first tried fried handpies while working together on *Feast* magazine, shooting a recipe written by our friend Alice Storey. They ended up being our nemeses, in a way: we made try after try attempting to capture the full glory of this deep-fried treat for the cover. In the end, they never went on the front of the magazine, but these little treats have since held a place in our hearts. The pastry is crunchy yet flaky, and the apricot is perfectly punctuated by the cardamom. – *Phoebe*

Makes 4

200 g (7 oz) apricot jam

200 g (7 oz) dried apricots, chopped

2 teaspoons vanilla bean paste

$1/8$ teaspoon ground cardamom, plus 1 teaspoon to dust

vegetable oil, for shallow-frying

110 g (4 oz) caster (superfine) sugar

Pastry

300 g ($10\frac{1}{2}$ oz/2 cups) plain (all-purpose) flour

$1/4$ teaspoon fine sea salt

100 g ($3\frac{1}{2}$ oz) cold unsalted butter, chopped

150 ml (5 fl oz) cold milk

2 teaspoons apple cider vinegar

For the pastry, combine the flour and salt in a bowl. Add the butter and roughly cut into the flour (there should still be some larger chunks of butter in the dough which will make the pastry lovely and flaky as it cooks). Add the milk and vinegar and stir to combine, then knead until the mixture just forms a dough. Shape into a disc, wrap in plastic wrap and chill for 3 hours.

Stir together the apricot jam, chopped apricots, vanilla bean paste and cardamom in a saucepan over low heat for 2–3 minutes until the jam has melted. Remove from the heat and leave to cool.

Divide the dough into 4 pieces. Roll out each one on a lightly floured work surface to a thickness of 3 mm ($1/8$ in). Cut out a 16 cm ($6\frac{1}{4}$ in) circle from each piece. Place 2 tablespoons of the apricot mixture in the centre of each circle then fold over to form a semi-circle, pinching the edges to seal. Repeat with the remaining pastry circles and mixture, then chill for 1 hour.

Heat 1 cm ($1/2$ in) of vegetable oil in a large heavy-based frying pan to 170°C (340°F). (If you don't have a kitchen thermometer you can test if the oil is hot enough by dropping in a small cube of bread; it should sizzle and turn brown in 20 seconds.) Cook the pies in two batches for 5 minutes, turning them over halfway through cooking, until the pastry is golden and cooked through.

Combine the sugar and cardamom in a bowl. Drain the pies on some paper towel and scatter over the cardamom sugar to serve.

Mixed berry handpies

The photograph of this pie was the screensaver on my phone for about six months I loved it so much. Whenever I'm making a pie, it's always a struggle to decide how to finish it. Do I do a thick distinctive lattice that always garners praise? An open top to allow the thick bubbling jam to spill over the sides? Or a careful plait that takes me to the tip of my pastry patience? Clearly, here I just couldn't decide, so did them all! Have fun with these lids and use your creativity to come up with your own designs. – Phoebe

Makes 4

2 × 435 g (15½ oz) frozen Careme vanilla bean pastry, thawed, or other bought sweet shortcrust rolled to a thickness of 3 mm (⅛ in)

500 g (1 lb 2 oz) mixed frozen berries, e.g. blueberries, raspberries and cranberries

2 ripe pears, peeled, cored and chopped

220 g (8 oz) caster (superfine) sugar

1 teaspoon natural vanilla extract

35 g (1¼ oz) vanilla custard powder

1 egg, lightly beaten

Cut four 14 cm (5½ in) rounds from one sheet of pastry and press into the bases and sides of four 10 cm (4 in) individual pie dishes. Chill for 30 minutes. Cut the remaining pastry into four, and then cut out as desired for the pie lids. You could cut the strips of pastry to make a lattice (see page 150), or use cookie cutters to cut out small holes from the lid, or cover the filling with rough triangle shapes. Place on a baking tray lined with baking paper and chill for 30 minutes.

Bring the berries, pears and sugar to a simmer in a saucepan over medium heat. Cook for 15 minutes or until syrupy. Remove from the heat and stir in the vanilla, then mix 4 tablespoons of the berry mixture with the custard powder until smooth. Return to the pan with the rest of the syrup and cook for 5 minutes, stirring, or until thickened. Remove from the heat and leave to cool completely.

Preheat the oven to 200°C (400°F). Divide the filling between the lined pie dishes and cover each one with a pastry lid, trimming the edges. Brush with the beaten egg and place on a baking tray. Bake for 10 minutes, then reduce the oven temperature to 180°C (350°F) and bake for a further 25 minutes or until golden. Cool to room temperature before serving.

Cherry jam handpies

My grandparents had a cherry orchard in Young, New South Wales, when I was little, so summers were always about huge boxes of fresh cherries that I would eat until I was almost ill. I love cherry jam for its sweet and tart flavour, which is the perfect balance in a pie, along with a beautiful buttery pastry. These pies remind me of the cherry Danishes I used to sneak after school if I had some spare pocket money – and my parents wondered why I didn't want to eat my big bowl of brown rice for dinner! – *Phoebe*

Makes 12

2 × 435 g (15½ oz) frozen Careme vanilla bean pastry, thawed, or other bought sweet shortcrust rolled to a thickness of 3 mm (⅛ in)

500 g (1 lb 2 oz) jar pitted morello cherries in syrup, drained, juice reserved (about 200 ml/ 7 fl oz)

110 g (4 oz) caster (superfine) sugar

2 tablespoons cornflour (cornstarch)

160 g (5½ oz/½ cup) cherry jam

1 egg, lightly beaten

icing (confectioners') sugar, to dust

Cut the pastry into 12 even squares. Place on two baking trays lined with baking paper and chill while you make the filling.

Bring the cherry juice and caster sugar to a simmer in a saucepan over medium–high heat, stirring to dissolve the sugar. Simmer for 15 minutes or until reduced by half. Mix 3 tablespoons of the syrup with the cornflour in a small bowl until smooth, then return to the saucepan along with the cherries and cherry jam. Simmer for a further 8 minutes or until the liquid is thick and glossy. Remove from the heat and leave to cool completely.

Preheat the oven to 180°C (350°F). Place 1 tablespoon of the cherry filling in the centre of each square and brush the edges with beaten egg. Fold over the pastry to make a rectangle and press the edges to seal with a fork. Cut a few small slits in the tops to allow the steam to escape, then brush with more beaten egg. Bake for 20 minutes or until golden and bubbling. Cool slightly, then dust with icing sugar to serve.

Almond, vanilla and raspberry handpies

I love how super-simple these pies are – hardly any ingredients for a great result. The best thing about handpies is that you really have an excuse not to share. There are some really good-quality store-bought puff pastries out there nowadays; just make sure you buy butter puff and not a margarine- or oil-based pastry. – *Phoebe*

Makes 4

250 g (9 oz) fresh raspberries

100 g (3½ oz) demerara sugar

1 vanilla bean, split lengthways and seeds scraped

2 teaspoons finely grated lemon zest

2 teaspoons lemon juice

2 sheets frozen butter puff pastry (total 330 g/ 11½ oz), thawed, and if needed, rolled to a thickness of 2 mm (⅛ in)

50 g (1¾ oz) almond meal

1 egg, lightly beaten

4 tablespoons flaked almonds

Preheat the oven to 200°C (400°F). Mix together the raspberries, sugar, vanilla seeds and lemon zest and juice in a bowl with a fork, lightly crushing some of the raspberries.

Cut each sheet of pastry into four equal squares and place four pieces on a baking tray lined with baking paper.

Stir the almond meal through the raspberry mixture and divide between the squares on the baking tray, leaving a 1 cm (½ in) border all round. Top with the remaining pastry squares, pressing the edges to seal. Brush with the beaten egg and scatter with the flaked almonds. Cook for 25–30 minutes until golden.

Chocolate and peanut butter brownie handpies

What about this pie?! Take a brownie (yes, please) and a pastry pie crust (yes, please) and marry them. When Phoebe cooked these little pies for the book shoot, I got excited. Very excited. They have a brownie texture with crisp pastry crunch and a salty punch from the peanut butter, all in a convenient single-serve handpie, which caused a bit of an issue for me as I ate one, and then ate another one – apparently the single serve didn't apply to me. – *Kirsten*

Makes 6

2 × 300 g (10½ oz) frozen Careme chocolate pastry, thawed, or other bought chocolate shortcrust rolled to a thickness of 3 mm (⅛ in)

80 g (2¾ oz) unsalted butter

200 g (7 oz) dark chocolate, chopped

1 tablespoon good-quality cocoa powder

2 tablespoons sunflower oil

150 g (5½ oz) soft brown sugar

1 teaspoon natural vanilla extract

2 eggs, plus 2 egg yolks

140 g (5 oz) crunchy peanut butter

100 g (3½ oz/⅔ cup) plain (all-purpose) flour

¼ teaspoon fine sea salt

1 tablespoon crushed peanuts and pinch of salt flakes, to scatter

Preheat the oven to 180°C (350°F). Line six 10 cm × 2 cm deep (4 in × 1½ in) oval pie dishes with pastry, trimming away any excess pastry. Line the pastry cases with baking paper and fill with baking beads (or uncooked rice or dried beans). Blind bake for 10 minutes or until slightly dry. Remove the baking paper and baking beads. Reduce the oven temperature to 160°C (320°F).

Put the butter, 150 g (5½ oz) of the chocolate and the cocoa powder in a saucepan over low heat, stirring until the chocolate has melted, then remove from the heat.

Whisk together the sunflower oil, sugar, vanilla, eggs and egg yolks, and the peanut butter until smooth. Mix in the flour and salt, then stir in the chocolate mixture and remaining chopped chocolate. Divide between the pie dishes and bake for 20 minutes or until cooked through but still fudgy in the centre. Cool to room temperature before scattering with the crushed peanuts and salt flakes and serving.

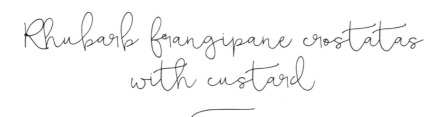

Rhubarb frangipane crostatas with custard

Crostatas are a great beginner's pie, as they can be a bit wonky and random and still look really cool – you just have to run with it. We both love adding herbs to desserts and the rosemary in this adds a really rich savoury element to the rhubarb and sweet almond frangipane. – *Phoebe*

Makes 6

2 × 435 g (15½ oz) frozen Careme vanilla bean pastry, thawed, or other bought sweet shortcrust rolled to a thickness of 3 mm (⅛ in)

250 g (9 oz) rhubarb, trimmed and cut into 6–10 cm (2½–4 in) lengths

2 teaspoons finely chopped rosemary leaves

150 g (5½ oz) caster (superfine) sugar

90 g (3 oz) unsalted butter, at room temperature

finely grated zest of 1 orange

2 teaspoons vanilla bean paste

1 egg

150 g (5½ oz) almond meal

3 teaspoons cornflour (cornstarch)

thick vanilla bean custard to serve

Cut out six 16 cm (6¼ in) circles from the pastry and lay them on three baking trays lined with baking paper. Chill while you make the filling.

Combine the rhubarb, rosemary and 70 g (2½ oz) of the sugar in a bowl. Set aside to macerate for 15 minutes. Preheat the oven to 200°C (400°F).

Beat the butter and the remaining 80 g (2¾ oz/ ⅓ cup) sugar until pale using an electric mixer. Beat in the orange zest and vanilla, then the egg. Finally, beat in the almond meal and cornflour.

Divide the frangipane mixture between the pastry circles (still on their trays), leaving a 2 cm (¾ in) border all the way round. Top with the macerated rhubarb and fold over the edges slightly to enclose. Bake for 15 minutes or until the pastry is golden and the rhubarb is tender. Cool slightly, then drizzle with custard to serve.

Tiramisu handpies

My mum, Debs, is a born entertainer. Growing up, our house was always the house to drop into just to say 'Hi', and the house for fantastic dinner parties. I loved knowing it was a dinner party night and loved all the 'special' food that would appear. I wanted to know the types of cheese my mum had bought for the cheese plates, I wanted to know what she was cooking for the main course, and I desperately wanted to be involved in the dessert-making. I always remember the excitement of a tiramisu. My job was to soak the Italian biscuits in the coffee and liqueur, just enough so they weren't dry but not too much that they completely fell apart in my hands. I took this job very seriously and have loved this dessert ever since. – Kirsten

Makes 6

250 g (9 oz) plain chocolate biscuits (cookies)

85 g (3 oz) unsalted butter, melted then cooled

2 teaspoons instant coffee granules

3 egg yolks

2 tablespoons caster (superfine) sugar

1 teaspoon vanilla bean paste

3 tablespoons pure icing (confectioners') sugar, sifted

250 g (9 oz) mascarpone cheese

250 ml (8½ fl oz/1 cup) thick (double/heavy) cream

2 teaspoons Marsala (optional)

1 tablespoon crushed cacao nibs to serve

2 teaspoons good-quality cocoa powder to serve

Pulse the biscuits in a food processor to coarse crumbs. Add the butter and pulse again to combine.

Press the crumb mixture into the bases of six 11 cm (4¼ in) pie dishes.

Stir to dissolve the coffee in 1 tablespoon of boiling water, then set aside.

Place the egg yolks and caster sugar in a heatproof bowl set over a saucepan of gently simmering water (make sure the bottom of the bowl doesn't touch the hot water). Whisk for 6 minutes or until the sugar has dissolved and the mixture is thick and pale. Transfer the mixture to the bowl of an electric mixer fitted with a whisk attachment, and whisk for 5 minutes or until cooled completely. Turn off the mixer and add the vanilla, icing sugar, mascarpone and cream, then whisk for 1–2 minutes until stiff peaks form – be careful not to overmix.

Halve the mixture and fold the coffee mixture through one portion. Fold the Marsala (if using) through the other half. Divide the coffee filling among the pastry cases and top with the other filling. Scatter with cacao nibs and cocoa to serve.

Pear, maple syrup and ginger handpies

This is as easy as they come! You don't even need to make separate pies in this recipe. We love the idea of rolling out two sheets of pastry, building neat little piles of sticky pear filling on one and then covering it with the other like a warm blanket on a cold night, and cooking. – *Kirsten*

Serves 12

3 hard, crisp pears, e.g. Beurré Bosc pears, peeled, cored and finely chopped

125 ml (4 fl oz/$\frac{1}{2}$ cup) maple syrup

20 g ($\frac{3}{4}$ oz) crystallised (candied) ginger, chopped

1 egg, lightly beaten with 1 tablespoon water

2 tablespoons demerara sugar

Pastry

400 g (14 oz/$2\frac{2}{3}$ cups) plain (all-purpose) flour

55 g (2 oz/$\frac{1}{4}$ cup) caster (superfine) sugar

$\frac{1}{4}$ teaspoon fine sea salt

250 g (9 oz) cold unsalted butter, cut into 2 cm ($\frac{3}{4}$ in) cubes

2 tablespoons apple cider vinegar mixed with 160 ml ($5\frac{1}{2}$ fl oz) cold water and 4 ice cubes

For the pastry, combine the flour, sugar and salt in a bowl. Add the butter pieces and toss to coat. Turn out onto a clean work surface and, using a pastry cutter (or flat-bladed knife), roughly cut the butter into the flour mixture (leave some large chunks of butter as this will help the pastry to become nice and flaky as it cooks).

Create a well in the centre of the flour mixture and add the vinegar water in 3 batches, working it in with your hands to form a rough dough (you may not need all of the water). Divide the dough into 2 pieces, one twice the size of the other. Shape each piece into a rough disc and wrap in plastic wrap. Chill for 3 hours.

Place the smaller piece of pastry on a lightly floured work surface and roll out to 32 cm × 26 cm ($12\frac{3}{4}$ in × $10\frac{1}{4}$ in) then place on a baking tray. Roll out the larger piece of pastry until it is 6 cm ($2\frac{1}{2}$ in) wider than the smaller piece all the way round and place on another baking tray. Chill for 1 hour.

Meanwhile, cook the pears with the maple syrup and ginger in a saucepan over medium heat, stirring occasionally, for 25 minutes or until softened. Remove from the heat and cool completely.

To make the pies, evenly space the filling in 6 portions over the smaller piece of pastry. Lay the larger rectangle over the top and press down around each mound of filling to seal into 6 rectangular pies. Using the edge of a ruler or a blunt knife press down between each pie to make an indentation. Brush with the egg wash and scatter with the demerara sugar, then chill for 30 minutes. Preheat the oven to 200°C (400°F).

Bake for 40 minutes or until the pastry is golden and the pies are cooked through. Cool slightly then use a knife to break them into individual pies.

S'more handpies

Growing up, I always loved the descriptions of s'mores in American novels. While we were occasionally allowed marshmallows with our mug of unsweetened cocoa, s'mores would definitely have been off limits! This is my take on those classic American campfire flavours. I took these to my partner Simon's house after the shoot and while we didn't sit around a fire singing camp songs, standing in the kitchen at midnight devouring them with a glass of red was, I think, just as satisfying. – Phoebe

Makes 6

250 g (9 oz) shortbread biscuits (cookies)

½ teaspoon ground ginger

70 g (2½ oz) unsalted butter, melted then cooled

200 g (7 oz) dark chocolate, chopped

200 ml (7 fl oz) pouring (single/light) cream

2 egg whites

150 g (5½ oz) caster (superfine) sugar

50 g (1¾ oz) white marshmallows, chopped

Pulse the biscuits and ginger in a food processor to fine crumbs. Add the butter and pulse again to combine.

Press the crumb mixture into the bases and sides of a six-hole 80 ml (2½ fl oz/⅓ cup) capacity muffin tin, then chill.

Put the chocolate in a heatproof bowl. Heat the cream in a microwave-safe jug in the microwave on high, or in a small saucepan over medium heat, until it reaches just below boiling point. Pour over the chocolate and stir until it forms a smooth, melted ganache. Divide among the muffin holes and chill for 2 hours or until set.

For the marshmallow topping, whisk the egg whites and sugar together in a heatproof bowl set over a saucepan of gently simmering water (make sure the bottom of the bowl doesn't touch the hot water). Whisk for 10 minutes until thick ribbons can be formed and the sugar has dissolved. Whisk in the marshmallows until dissolved, then transfer to the bowl of an electric mixer and whisk until cooled completely. Dollop on top of the chocolate ganache and, using a kitchen blowtorch, gently caramelise the marshmallow. If you don't have a blowtorch place them under a very hot grill (broiler) for 1–2 minutes. Serve immediately.

Note To make it easier to release the pies from the tins, you could cut twelve 1 cm (½ in) thick strips of baking paper and place them in a cross on the base of the muffin tins before you press in the crumb. Use the cross to help lift the cooked pies out of the tins.

Baby stack pies

I have such a soft spot for stack pie – a Southern American pie that came about when churchgoers took pies to functions, and stacked them up on top of each other as a mode of transport. They sliced them like a layer cake to serve. It was really more like a Tupperware solution than a considered dessert. This recipe uses a traditional chess pie, but I've replaced the frosting with thick layers of sour cream and raspberries to cut through the sweetness. It is dedicated to our fellow Feasties at the magazine – Anita, Lara, Dan, Alix, Rachel, Eloise and Dylan – who share our love of this heroic pie. – *Phoebe*

Serves 4

2 × 435 g (15½ oz) frozen Careme vanilla bean pastry, thawed, or other bought sweet shortcrust rolled to a thickness of 3 mm (⅛ in)

60 g (2 oz) unsalted butter, melted then cooled completely to prevent splitting

220 g (8 oz) caster (superfine) sugar

1 tablespoon fine polenta

2 eggs

2 tablespoons pouring (single/light) cream

2 teaspoons apple cider vinegar

½ teaspoon vanilla bean paste

160 g (5½ oz/⅔ cup) sour cream

2 tablespoons crushed freeze-dried raspberries to serve

Cut out six 15 cm (6 in) rounds from the pastry and press into the base and sides of six 11 cm (4¼ in) fluted tart tins. Trim the edges and chill for 2 hours.

Preheat the oven to 200°C (400°F). Line the pastry cases with baking paper and fill with baking beads (or uncooked rice or dried beans). Cook for 20 minutes or until the pastry is light golden. Remove the baking paper and baking beads then cook for a further 5 minutes or until golden and dry. Remove from the oven and leave to cool. Reduce the oven temperature to 150°C (300°F).

Whisk together the butter, sugar, polenta, eggs, cream, vinegar and vanilla in a bowl, then divide among the pastry cases. Place on a baking tray and bake for 18 minutes or until just set. Allow to cool completely, then chill for 2 hours until cold.

Spread the top of each tart with a heaped tablespoon of sour cream then stack three on top of each other to make two stack pies. Scatter with the freeze-dried raspberries and cut in half to serve.

Chocolate and cherry pithiviers

A French pithivier is a round enclosed pie made from buttery puff pastry. It has the appearance of a slight hump in the middle and the edges are pinched together to seal. Our chosen 'hump' of filling in these little pies is the very popular cherry and chocolate combination. – Kirsten

Makes 12

6 sheets frozen butter puff pastry (total 1 kg/ 2 lb 3 oz), thawed, and if needed, rolled to a thickness of 2 mm (¹/₈ in)

100 g (3½ oz) dark chocolate, chopped

100 g (3½ oz) almond meal

1 tablespoon good-quality cocoa powder

160 g (5½ oz/½ cup) cherry jam

150 g (5½ oz) soft brown sugar

1 egg, plus 1 egg yolk

25 g (1 oz) unsalted butter, softened

1 egg, beaten with 1 tablespoon water

Line two baking trays with baking paper and cut out twelve 9 cm (3½ in) rounds of pastry and twelve 10 cm (4 in) rounds. Place the pastry on the trays, then score lines across the larger rounds, about 6 mm (¼ in) apart and leaving a 1 cm (½ in) border all the way round. Place the pastry on their trays in the freezer.

Meanwhile, place the chocolate, almond meal and cocoa powder in a food processor and whiz to combine. Add the jam, sugar, egg and egg yolk, and butter and whiz again to form a thick paste. Preheat the oven to 200°C (400°F).

Remove the trays from the freezer and place heaped tablespoons of the filling in the centre of the 9 cm (3½ in) rounds leaving about a 1 cm (½ in) border all the way round. Brush the edges with the egg wash and place the larger pastry rounds over the top, scored sides facing up. Press the edges to seal, then brush the tops with more egg wash. Place in the oven for 20 minutes or until golden and cooked through.

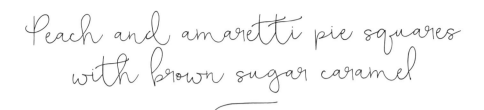

Peach and amaretti pie squares with brown sugar caramel

Peach and amaretti biscuits is a fantastic Italian pairing, as if I didn't like amaretti biscuits enough already! If this is for a dinner party, serve the pies with a thick dollop of mascarpone cheese as well, to up the indulgence factor. – *Phoebe*

Makes 4

1 sheet frozen butter puff pastry (total 165 g/5¾ oz), thawed, and if needed, rolled to a thickness of 2 mm (⅛ in), cut into 4 squares

2 white peaches, stones removed, thinly sliced

4 amaretti biscuits (cookies), crumbled

1 tablespoon soft brown sugar dissolved in 1 tablespoon boiling water

Brown sugar caramel

50 g (1¾ oz) soft brown sugar

50 g (1¾ oz) unsalted butter

60 ml (2 fl oz/¼ cup) pouring (single/light) cream

Preheat the oven to 200°C (400°F). Place the pastry squares on a baking tray lined with baking paper and scatter over the crumbled amaretti biscuits, leaving a 1 cm (½ in) border all the way round.

Divide the peach slices among the squares. Brush the sugar water over the peach then bake for 18 minutes or until golden.

Meanwhile, for the caramel, heat all the ingredients in a saucepan and cook over medium heat, stirring for 5 minutes or until golden and thickened. Cool to room temperature, then drizzle over the squares to serve.

Note If amaretti biscuits aren't your thing, use ginger nuts (gingersnaps) or shortbread for the base and they will work just as well.

Glazed apple and cinnamon handpies

These handpies are like apple pie and a doughnut in one. The flaky fried pastry and caramelised apples is an absolutely wicked combination, and the crunchy Krispy Kreme-style glaze is the perfect finish. I took these to a picnic and they were devoured in minutes. They don't have a great shelf life, so make sure they're eaten on the day you make them (it won't be hard). – *Phoebe*

Makes 6

600 g (1 lb 5 oz/4 cups) plain (all-purpose) flour

¼ teaspoon fine sea salt

200 g (7 oz) cold unsalted butter, chopped

300 ml (10 fl oz) cold milk

1 tablespoon apple cider vinegar

Apple filling

40 g (1½ oz) unsalted butter

250 g (9 oz) dark muscovado sugar

1 teaspoon ground cinnamon

4 apples (about 650 g/1 lb 4 oz), peeled, cored and sliced into thin rounds

1 egg, lightly beaten

vegetable oil, for frying

Doughnut glaze

90 g (3 oz/¾ cup) pure icing (confectioners') sugar

25 g (1 oz) unsalted butter, melted

1½ tablespoons milk

½ teaspoon ground cinnamon

Combine the flour and salt in a bowl. Add the butter and roughly cut into the flour (leave some larger chunks of butter in the dough, as this will make the pastry lovely and flaky as it cooks). Add the milk and vinegar and stir to combine, then knead until the mixture just forms a dough. Shape into a disc, wrap in plastic wrap and chill for 3 hours.

For the apple filling, melt the butter in a saucepan with the sugar, cinnamon and 2 teaspoons of water over low heat. Cook the apples in batches for 10 minutes or until tender. Remove the apples using a slotted spoon and leave to cool. Cook the syrup for a further minute or until very thick and reduced. Cool completely.

Roll out the pastry on a lightly floured work surface. Cut out six 10 cm (4 in) circles and six 11 cm (4¼ in) circles. Place about 4 apple slices in the centre of each smaller circle, and top with 1 teaspoon of the reduced syrup. Brush the edges with the beaten egg, then place the larger rounds over the top, pressing the edges together to seal.

Half-fill a deep, heavy-based saucepan or deep-fryer with vegetable oil and heat to 170°C (340°F). (If you don't have a kitchen thermometer you can test if the oil is hot enough by dropping in a small cube of bread; it should sizzle and turn brown in 20 seconds.) Working in 3 batches, cook the pies for 4 minutes on each side until golden and cooked through. Remove them using a slotted spoon and drain on paper towel. Leave to cool slightly.

To make the glaze, whisk together all the ingredients in a bowl until smooth. Dip the pies in the glaze and drain them on a wire rack set over a tray. Serve while still warm.

Tahini and honey handpies

When I was a kid, tahini and honey sandwiched between thick rice cakes was a regular snack. Despite rolling my eyes and grumbling about it then, I now love this flavour combination. This recipe is inspired by a food trend I'm also loving: decadent vegan chocolate, rich with coconut oil, nuts and natural sweeteners. I used real chocolate in mine, as I couldn't resist, but I love these 'healthy' flavours with the buttery pastry. – Phoebe

Makes 4

4 tablespoons tahini

220 g (8 oz) blanched almonds

200 g (7 oz) white chocolate, chopped

2 tablespoons coconut oil

40 g (1½ oz) desiccated (dried shredded) coconut

2 tablespoons honey to serve

1 tablespoon black sesame seeds to serve

Pastry

200 g (7 oz/1⅓ cups) plain (all-purpose) flour

55 g (2 oz/¼ cup) caster (superfine) sugar

¼ teaspoon fine sea salt

125 g (4½ oz) cold unsalted butter, cut into 2 cm (¾ in) cubes

2 teaspoons apple cider vinegar mixed with 80 ml (2½ fl oz/⅓ cup) cold water and 4 ice cubes

To make the pastry, combine the flour, sugar and salt in a bowl. Add the butter pieces and toss to coat. Turn out onto a clean work surface and, using a pastry cutter (or flat-bladed knife), roughly cut the butter into the flour mixture (leave some large chunks of butter as this will help the pastry to become nice and flaky as it cooks).

Create a well in the centre of the flour mixture and add the vinegar water in 3 batches, working it in with your hands to form a rough dough (you may not need all of the water). Shape the dough into a rough disc and wrap in plastic wrap. Chill for 3 hours.

Roll out the pastry on a lightly floured work surface to a circle with a thickness of 3 mm (⅛ in). Line four 10 cm × 2 cm deep (4 in × ¾ in) oval pie dishes with the pastry. Trim the edges and chill for 2 hours.

Preheat the oven to 200°C (400°F). Line the pastry cases with baking paper and fill with baking beads (or uncooked rice or dried beans). Cook for 20 minutes or until the pastry is light golden. Remove the paper and baking beads, then bake for a further 5 minutes or until the pastry is golden and dry to the touch. Remove from the oven and leave to cool completely.

Meanwhile, whiz the tahini, almonds, chocolate, coconut oil and desiccated coconut in a food processor until thick and smooth.

Divide the filling among the cooled cases and chill for 2 hours until firm and set. Drizzle with honey and scatter with black sesame seeds to serve.

Honey and ginger custard brûlée pie

This pie sent our family and friends into a frenzy, resulting in text messages, phone calls and demands for more. A text from my brother-in-law, Lewis, just read, 'O M freaking G', and my little sister, Ali, inhaled two slices in seconds. Meanwhile across town, Kirsten's partner, Georgie, proclaimed, 'I am so happy, I am crying.' Inspired by the amazing tiny ginger brûlée morsels from Sydney's Bourke Street Bakery, this pie is creamy and crunchy with a delicious hit of spice. If you don't have a kitchen blowtorch, put your pie under a piping hot grill (broiler) until nice and caramelised. – *Phoebe*

Serves 8

370 g (13 oz) ginger nut biscuits (cookies) (gingersnaps)

100 g (3½ oz) unsalted butter, melted then cooled

175 g (6 oz/½ cup) honey

2 teaspoons vanilla bean paste

600 ml (20½ fl oz) pouring (single/light) cream

110 g (4 oz/½ cup) chopped crystallised (candied) ginger

6 egg yolks

3 teaspoons cornflour (cornstarch)

55 g (2 oz/¼ cup) caster (superfine) sugar

Pulse the biscuits in a food processor to crumbs. Add the butter and pulse again to combine.

Press the crumb mixture into the base and side of a 24 cm (9½ in) loose-based fluted tart tin. Freeze for 1 hour.

Put the honey, vanilla, cream and ginger in a saucepan over medium heat and bring to just below boiling point, stirring to combine. Set aside to infuse for 30 minutes.

Preheat the oven to 150°C (300°F). Whisk the egg yolks with the cornflour in a heatproof bowl until pale. Return the cream mixture to a simmer, then pour over the egg yolks and stir to combine. Transfer to a clean saucepan and cook over medium–low heat, stirring constantly, for 6 minutes or until thickened. Strain through a fine sieve into a clean bowl, pressing down to extract as much flavour from the ginger as possible.

Pour into the biscuit case, then bake for 30 minutes or until it is set at the edge but with a distinct wobble in the centre. Remove from the oven and cool to room temperature, then chill for 4 hours or until completely cold.

Scatter the top with the sugar, then caramelise with a kitchen blowtorch before serving.

Chocolate and bitter marmalade pie with burnt chocolate meringue

This beautiful creation was partly inspired by a cracking dessert we had at Ester restaurant in Chippendale, Sydney. Ester reached local Instagram fame with a dessert on their menu called the 'Burnt Pav' – a soft pillow of meringue cooked in a hot wood-fired oven until beautifully charred on the outside and puffy and light in the middle. – *Kirsten*

Serves 12

300 g (10½ oz) frozen Careme chocolate pastry, thawed, or other bought chocolate shortcrust rolled to a thickness of 3 mm (⅛ in)

500 ml (17 fl oz/2 cups) pouring (single/light) cream

300 g (10½ oz) dark chocolate, chopped

6 eggs, separated

310 g (11 oz/1⅓ cups caster (superfine) sugar

35 g (1¼ oz) cornflour (cornstarch)

170 g (6 oz) Seville orange marmalade

35 g (1¼ oz) good-quality cocoa powder

Preheat the oven to 200°C (400°F). Line a 26 cm × 17 cm (10¼ in × 6¾ in) pie dish with the pastry, then line the pastry case with baking paper and fill with baking beads (or uncooked rice or dried beans). Bake for 15 minutes, then remove the baking beads and paper and cook for a further 10 minutes or until the pastry is dry to the touch. Remove from the oven and leave to cool completely. Reduce the oven temperature to 180°C (350°F).

Melt the cream and chocolate in a saucepan over medium heat, stirring, until the chocolate has melted. Remove from the heat.

Whisk the egg yolks, 145 g (5 oz/⅔ cup) of the sugar and the cornflour together until pale. Pour the chocolate mixture gradually over the egg mixture and whisk to combine. Return to a clean saucepan and cook over medium heat, whisking constantly, for 5 minutes or until thickened and smooth. Remove from the heat and leave to cool.

Spread the marmalade over the pastry base. Pour in the chocolate and cream mixture and smooth over the surface. Bake for 20 minutes or until the custard is just set, with a gentle wobble in the centre. Cool to room temperature, and then chill for 3 hours or until firm.

When ready to serve, whisk the egg whites with a pinch of salt to soft peaks using an electric mixer. Add the remaining sugar, 1 tablespoon at a time, until stiff peaks form. Whisk in the cocoa, then spoon over the pie. Use a kitchen blowtorch on the meringue until dark and charred, or put your pie under a piping hot grill (broiler).

Lemon curd, ricotta and poppy seed pie

Poppy seed and citrus are just meant to hang out together – everyone knows a good ol' orange and poppy seed cake, but in this recipe we wanted to swap the orange for lemon in the form of a great curd. The savoury ricotta cheese with the sweet and sour lemon curd makes a lovely light pie with a great biscuit base. – Kirsten

Serves 8

325 g (11½ oz) digestive biscuits (cookies)

125 g (4½ oz) unsalted butter, melted then cooled

350 g (12½ oz) fresh ricotta cheese

250 g (9 oz) cream cheese, softened

75 g (2¾ oz) caster (superfine) sugar

1 teaspoon cornflour (cornstarch)

2 eggs

200 g (7 oz) good-quality lemon curd

3 teaspoons poppy seeds

Preheat the oven to 200°C (400°F). Pulse the biscuits in a food processor to crumbs. Add the butter and pulse again to combine.

Press the crumb mixture into the base and side of a 22 cm (8¾ in) fluted tart tin, and bake for 10 minutes or until golden. Remove from the oven and leave to cool. Reduce the oven temperature to 160°C (320°F).

Put the ricotta and cream cheeses in the food processor with the sugar, cornflour and eggs and process until smooth. Add the lemon curd and pulse to combine, then stir through the poppy seeds. Pour the mixture into the prepared biscuit base and cook for 35 minutes or until set but with a slight wobble in the centre. Cool to room temperature, then chill for 2 hours or until cold.

Tamarind and lime pie with salted cashew praline

We love pairing sour with salt. This recipe is like all the goodness of a margarita, in a pie. It might sound like a bit of a funky combo but it really works. It's all about the sour from the tamarind and lime, with the sweet and salty praline. Don't worry about the sharpness in this pie: it is completely balanced by the sugar, and it's just like having a cracking good lemon pie. – *Kirsten*

Serves 12

435 g (15½ oz) frozen Careme vanilla bean pastry, thawed, or other bought sweet shortcrust rolled to a thickness of 3 mm (⅛ in)

juice of 2 limes

80 ml (2½ fl oz/⅓ cup) tamarind concentrate

6 eggs

220 g (8 oz) caster (superfine) sugar

250 ml (8½ fl oz/1 cup) thick (double/heavy) cream

Salted cashew praline

oil spray, for greasing

150 g (5½ oz) caster (superfine) sugar

3 tablespoons roughly chopped roasted cashews

1 teaspoon sea salt flakes

Line a 26 cm × 26 cm × 3 cm deep (10¼ in × 10¼ in × 1¼ in) pie dish with the pastry and press into the sides. Chill in the freezer for 30 minutes.

Preheat the oven to 180°C (350°F). Trim away any excess pastry, then line the case with baking paper and fill with baking beads (or uncooked rice or dried beans). Place on a baking tray and cook for 15 minutes. Remove the paper and baking beads then cook for a further 10 minutes or until the pastry looks golden and feels dry to the touch. Set aside to cool. Reduce the oven temperature to 160°C (320°F).

Whisk the lime juice, tamarind, eggs, sugar and cream in a bowl until combined, then leave to stand for 5 minutes. Pour the tamarind filling into the pastry case and bake for about 25 minutes or until the filling has just set. Cool to room temperature then refrigerate until cold.

To make the salted cashew praline, line a baking tray with foil and grease it lightly with oil spray. Place the sugar in a clean saucepan over medium-high heat. Cook, without stirring, for 3 minutes or until the sugar starts to caramelise. Swirl the pan occasionally for a further 3 minutes or until the caramel is dark golden. Add the cashews and swirl to coat them in the caramel, then pour over the tray in a single layer. Scatter with the salt flakes and set aside for 30 minutes until hard. Break the praline into large shards and serve with the pie.

Peach Melba ice cream pie

Peach Melba is one of those Aussie classics that will just never get old. It is the absolute taste of summer with amazing peaches, tangy raspberries and a really simple vanilla ice cream. This recipe is so easy, but it still looks impressive. While I've served it with beautiful fresh peaches, the granita is actually made with tinned ones. I secretly like tinned peaches and they were a staple growing up in our house when the fruit trees weren't in season. If we got a bowl of peaches and ice cream for dessert, it was a great day. – Phoebe

Serves 8

220 g (8 oz) caster (superfine) sugar

150 g (5½ oz) frozen raspberries

240 g (8½ oz) tinned peaches in syrup, drained

650 ml (22 fl oz) vanilla ice cream, softened

fresh peaches, to serve

Sponge

150 g (5½ oz) unsalted butter, softened

80 g (2¾ oz/⅓ cup) caster (superfine) sugar

2 eggs

1 teaspoon natural vanilla extract

2 tablespoons plain Greek-style yoghurt or sour cream

150 g (5½ oz/1 cup) self-raising flour, sifted

To make the granita, combine the sugar and 500 ml (17 fl oz/2 cups) of water in a saucepan over medium heat, and stir until the sugar dissolves. Remove from the heat and stir in the raspberries and tinned peaches. Leave to cool completely, then blitz in a food processor until finely chopped but still with some chunks. Pour into a 30 cm × 20 cm × 3 cm deep (12 in × 8 in × 1¼ in) container and freeze for 2 hours, then rake with a fork to agitate the mixture. Refreeze and repeat the process twice more.

For the sponge, preheat the oven to 160°C (320°F). Grease the base of a 22 cm × 4 cm deep (8¾ in × 1½ in) pie dish. Place the butter and sugar in the bowl of an electric mixer and beat until thick and pale. Add the eggs, one at a time, beating well after each addition. Beat in the vanilla and yoghurt, then fold in the flour. Spread into the prepared dish and bake for 40 minutes or until golden and cooked through, and a skewer inserted in the centre comes out clean. Leave to cool to room temperature.

Spread the ice cream over the cooled sponge and freeze for 2 hours or until frozen. Serve with the granita and slices of fresh peach.

Yin and yang

In some ways, Kirsten and I are like these pies: yin and yang. We always have different ideas and think about things in different ways, but somehow we just work together. We both love a bit of symmetry. We loved the idea of two striking contrasting pies in black and white and panna cotta was the perfect easy filling. These are great summer pies to put in a cooler bag chocked with ice blocks to take on a picnic, or equally, you can serve them as an elegant end to a dinner party. – *Phoebe*

Serves 16
Makes 2 × 18 cm (7 in) pies

Vanilla panna cotta

435 g (15½ oz) frozen Careme vanilla bean pastry, thawed, or other sweet shortcrust rolled to a thickness of 3 mm (⅛ in)

3 titanium-strength gelatine leaves

600 ml (20½ fl oz) pouring (single/light) cream

250 ml (8½ fl oz/1 cup) thick (double/heavy) cream

110 g (4 oz) caster (superfine) sugar

2 teaspoons vanilla bean paste

icing (confectioners') sugar, to dust

Chocolate panna cotta

300 g (10½ oz) frozen Careme chocolate shortcrust pastry, thawed, or other bought chocolate shortcrust rolled to a thickness of 3 mm (⅛ in)

3 titanium-strength gelatine leaves

600 ml (20½ fl oz) pouring (single/light) cream

110 g (4 oz) caster (superfine) sugar

200 g (7 oz) good-quality dark chocolate, finely chopped

good-quality cocoa powder, to dust

Line an 18 cm (7 in) pie dish with the vanilla pastry, trimming away any excess. Line another 18 cm (7 in) pie dish with the chocolate pastry, again trimming away any excess. Chill for 30 minutes.

Preheat the oven to 200°C (400°F). Line each pie dish with baking paper and fill with baking beads (or uncooked rice or dried beans). Place the pie dishes on a large baking tray and cook for 15 minutes or until just dry, then remove the baking beads and paper, and bake for a further 10 minutes or until the vanilla pastry is golden and dry and the chocolate pastry is dry to the touch. Leave to cool completely.

For the vanilla panna cotta, place the gelatine leaves in a bowl of cold water for 5 minutes. Put the creams, caster sugar and vanilla in a saucepan over medium heat and bring to just below boiling point, stirring to dissolve the sugar. Remove from the heat. Squeeze any excess water from the gelatine and add the gelatine to the cream mixture, stirring until dissolved. Strain through a fine sieve into a clean bowl and cool to room temperature, then pour into the cooked vanilla pastry case. Chill for 3 hours until set. Dust with the icing sugar to serve.

For the chocolate panna cotta, place the gelatine leaves in a bowl of cold water for 5 minutes. Put the cream and sugar in a saucepan over medium heat and bring to just below boiling point, stirring to dissolve the sugar. Place the chocolate in a heatproof bowl and pour over the hot cream mixture. Stir until completely melted and combined. Squeeze any excess water from the gelatine and add the gelatine to the chocolate mixture, stirring until dissolved. Strain through a fine sieve into a clean bowl and cool to room temperature, then pour into the cooked chocolate pastry case. Chill for 3 hours until set. Dust with the cocoa to serve.

Salted peanut banffy pie

We call this banoffee pie 'the banffy pie' because my mum, Cathy, just couldn't get her head around 'banoffee' and settled on 'banffy' instead. What can we say? It stuck. Banffy pie is always a crowd-pleaser and the addition of some crunchy, salted peanuts gives this pie a perfect sweet and salty balance. – *Phoebe*

Serves 8

320 g (11½ oz) shortbread biscuits (cookies)

70 g (2½ oz) unsalted butter, melted then cooled

675 g (1½ lb) dulce de leche

2 ripe bananas

80 ml (2½ fl oz/⅓ cup) thick (double/heavy) cream

250 ml (8½ fl oz/1 cup) pouring (single/light) cream

100 g (3½ oz) salted roasted peanuts, chopped

good-quality cocoa powder, to dust

You can make your own dulce de leche by boiling two 395 g (14 oz) tins of sweetened condensed milk, if you prefer. Remove and discard the labels from the tins, then make two holes in the lid of each using a tin opener. Place the tins in a saucepan, open side up, and fill the saucepan with cold water to about 1 cm (½ in) below the top of the tins. Bring to the boil over high heat, then reduce the heat to medium–low and simmer for 3 hours. Keep topping up the water. Carefully remove the tins and leave to cool, then open the tins and scoop out the caramel.

Pulse the biscuits in a food processor to fine crumbs. Add the butter and pulse again to combine.

Press the crumb mixture into the base and side of an 18 cm × 3 cm deep (7 in × 1¼ in) pie dish.

Spread the dulce de leche over the base and chill for 1 hour until firm.

Peel and slice the bananas, and lay the slices on top of the dulce de leche. Whisk the creams together until they form stiff peaks, then dollop over the banana. Scatter with the peanuts and dust with the cocoa to serve.

Coffee chess pie

Chess pie is a classic Southern American pie made from sugar, butter and eggs.
It forms the base of one of my all-time favourites: Baby stack pies on page 105.
I usually make my chess pies using polenta and vinegar to stabilise the filling, and
I'm such a fan of the coffee and chocolate combination in this version. The texture
is smooth and fudgy, and there is just enough coffee to cut through the sugar.
My friend Shannon is one of the healthiest people I know and she loves this pie.
I'm not telling her it's also called sugar pie. – Phoebe

Serves 8

400 g (14 oz) plain chocolate biscuits (cookies)

85 g (3 oz) unsalted butter, melted then cooled

Filling

220 g (8 oz) caster (superfine) sugar

3 eggs

80 g (2¾ oz) fine polenta

60 ml (2 fl oz/¼ cup) strong coffee

100 ml (3½ fl oz) thickened (whipping) cream

60 g (2 oz) unsalted butter, melted then cooled

2 teaspoons natural vanilla extract

Pulse the biscuits in a food processor to fine
crumbs. Add the butter and pulse again to combine.
Press into the base and side of a 23 cm (9 in)
loose-based fluted tart tin. Chill while you make
the filling.

Preheat the oven to 160°C (320°F). For the filling,
whisk together the sugar, eggs, polenta, coffee,
cream, butter and vanilla. Pour into the biscuit
base. Bake for 50 minutes or until the edge is set but
there is still a gentle wobble in the centre. Cool
completely to room temperature, then chill for
2 hours or until cold.

Lemon shaker pie

Lemons, to me, are such an essential ingredient in cooking; they draw out the flavours from other foods, they season and balance, they cut through any richness, and they can be utilised whole, like preserved lemons. I remember the first time Phoebe cooked this recipe: I watched her thinly slice the whole lemons and sit them, covered in sugar, overnight. I have to admit I didn't really believe in the recipe and thought it would be highly unlikely that I would really love the result. Well, I was wrong. This is like the 'impossible pie'. The result is an amazing lemon marmalade that forms from the lemons macerating. A thin layer of jammy, sticky lemon with a beautiful pastry base. If you are as big a fan of lemons as I am, then give this one a go. – Kirsten

Serves 8

2 lemons, thinly sliced

440 g (14 oz) caster (superfine) sugar

60 g (2 oz) unsalted butter, melted then cooled

3 eggs, lightly beaten

cream to serve

Pastry

200 g (7 oz/1⅓ cups) plain (all-purpose) flour

3 tablespoons caster (superfine) sugar

pinch of fine sea salt

125 g (4½ oz) cold unsalted butter, chopped

2 teaspoons apple cider vinegar mixed with 80 ml (2½ fl oz/⅓ cup) cold water and 4 ice cubes

Place the lemons and sugar in a bowl and stir to combine. Cover with plastic wrap and set aside at room temperature overnight.

For the pastry, combine the flour, sugar and salt in a bowl. Add the butter pieces and toss to coat. Turn out onto a clean work surface and, using a pastry cutter (or flat-bladed knife), cut the butter into the flour until coarsely combined (leave some large chunks of butter in the mixture as this will help the pastry to become nice and flaky as it cooks).

Create a well in the centre of the flour mixture and add the vinegar water in 3 batches, working it in with your hands to form a rough dough (you may not need all of the water). Shape into a disc, wrap in plastic wrap and chill for 3 hours or overnight with the lemons.

Roll out the pastry on a lightly floured work surface to 36 cm × 30 cm (14½ in × 12 in) and use it to line the base and sides of a 32 cm × 25 cm (12¾ in × 10 in) baking dish. Chill for 30 minutes.

Preheat the oven to 160°C (320°F). Combine the butter and eggs in a bowl with the lemon mixture and stir to combine. Pour into the pastry case and bake for 40 minutes or until the pastry is golden and cooked, and the filling has set but still has a gentle wobble in the centre. Cool completely, then chill until cold. Serve with cream.

Coconut pie with watermelon and mint

I think when we're talking about pie, people think of hot, cooked, pastry, fruit, chocolate, caramel etc. So we wanted to broaden that thought process and give you some great light and summery recipes, that don't necessarily need to be cooked and would be considered great go-to warm-weather desserts. This one is packed with the usual summer suspects: coconut, watermelon and mint. I love the combination of the creamy coconut with the icy sorbet. – *Kirsten*

Serves 10

3 titanium-strength gelatine leaves

500 ml (17 fl oz/2 cups) thickened (whipping) cream

400 ml (13½ fl oz) coconut cream

100 g (3½ oz) caster (superfine) sugar

watermelon sorbet to serve

3 tablespoons coconut flakes to serve

2 tablespoons fresh mint leaves to serve

Base

250 g (9 oz) shortbread or digestive biscuits (cookies)

70 g (2½ oz) unsalted butter, melted then cooled

50 g (1¾ oz) desiccated (dried shredded) coconut

pinch of fine sea salt

For the base, whiz the shortbread in a food processor to fine crumbs. Add the butter, coconut and salt, and pulse to combine. Press into the base of a 23 cm × 4 cm deep (9½ in × 1½ in) pie dish and chill until needed.

Place the gelatine leaves in a bowl of cold water and set aside for 5 minutes to soften. Heat the cream, coconut cream and sugar in a saucepan over medium heat, stirring to dissolve the sugar. Bring to just below boiling point then remove from the heat. Squeeze any excess water from the gelatine and add the gelatine to the cream mixture, stirring until dissolved. Strain through a fine sieve, then pour over the chilled coconut shortbread base. Chill for 4 hours or until set, then serve with scoops of watermelon sorbet, and scatter over the coconut flakes and mint leaves.

Note If you can't find watermelon sorbet, use something tropical – mango, pineapple or berry would work well.

Baked ricotta, orange blossom and date pie

This pie is very close to being my absolute favourite in the book. I love the classic Middle Eastern pairing of orange blossom and dates. There is a natural sweetness to the dates that means the pie filling doesn't need to be overly sweet. I also love the pattern we created on top of the pie. We had seen a photo of a cheesecake a while ago, which at first glance looked as though its filling had been piped into the pastry case in a circular fashion and then baked to create a beautiful tan-brown top on it. Then we realised it wasn't piping that had created the pattern but rather turning the cheesecake upside down straight out of the oven onto a circular wire rack to cool. We couldn't turn our pie upside down because of the biscuit crumbs, so we decided to put a wire rack on top of the pie and weigh it down to create its distinct criss-cross pattern. Of course, this is not an essential step in the recipe but I think it creates such a visual talking point you'd be crazy not to. – Kirsten

Serves 8

300 g (10½ oz) shortbread biscuits (cookies)

80 g (2¾ oz) unsalted butter, melted then cooled

500 g (1 lb 2 oz) firm fresh ricotta cheese

250 g (9 oz) cream cheese, at room temperature

170 g (6 oz/¾ cup) caster (superfine) sugar

2 eggs

2 teaspoons orange blossom water

2 teaspoons natural vanilla extract

8 dates, pitted and chopped

Pulse the biscuits in a food processor to fine crumbs. Add the butter and pulse again to combine.

Press the crumb mixture into the base and side of a 17 cm (6¾ in) pie dish. Chill while you make the filling.

Clean the processor then whiz the ricotta, cream cheese and sugar until smooth. Add the eggs, orange blossom water and vanilla and whiz to combine.

Preheat the oven to 180°C (350°F). Scatter the dates over the chilled biscuit base, then spread the ricotta mixture over the top. Bake for 50 minutes or until a dark golden colour and firm to the touch. Turn off the oven and leave to cool in the oven for 30 minutes with the door ajar.

Remove from the oven, and press a wire rack firmly over the cake while it is still warm to make indentations on the surface. Weigh it down with a tin or your tub of baking beads. Leave to cool to room temperature, then chill for 2 hours or until cold.

Spiced mango ice cream pie

This is like a fancy mango lassi pie. Think of that beautifully icy drink that you order at Indian restaurants, thick with blended mango and lightly spiced with cardamom. To me, cardamom and tropical fruit are meant to hang out together. If used properly and with some restraint it can provide one of the most intriguing flavour profiles; you can't always put your finger on what exactly it is but you definitely like it. This pie is a great summer option – and I don't know anyone who doesn't like an ice cream pie. – Kirsten

Serves 8

500 g (1 lb 2 oz) store-bought sponge cake

600 g (1 lb 5 oz) vanilla ice cream, softened

1 teaspoon ground cardamom

2 mangoes, peeled and sliced

Spiced syrup

4 cardamom pods, lightly crushed

110 g (4 oz) caster (superfine) sugar

1 vanilla bean, split lengthways and seeds scraped

Cut the sponge into 1 cm (½ in) thick slices and use them to line the base of a 30 cm × 20 cm (12 in × 8 in) pie dish.

Combine the ice cream and ground cardamom in a bowl, and spread out over the sponge. Freeze for 2 hours or until firm.

For the spiced syrup, place the cardamom pods, sugar, vanilla pod and seeds, and 125ml (4 fl oz/ ½ cup) of water in a saucepan over medium heat, stirring to dissolve the sugar. Bring to the boil and simmer for 1 minute, then remove from the heat and leave to cool completely.

Bring the ice cream sponge out of the freezer about 20 minutes before serving. Arrange the mango slices over the ice cream, then drizzle with the spiced syrup.

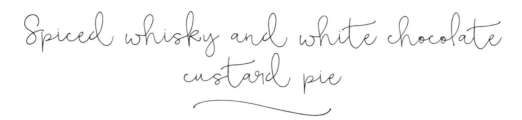

Spiced whisky and white chocolate custard pie

I started drinking whisky in New York and haven't stopped since. I love the robust addition of whisky to a creamy custard pie. This is definitely a 'grown-ups' pie, and is perfect for a winter dinner party, or your next Thanksgiving showstopper. – Phoebe

Serves 8

2 tablespoons vanilla custard powder

1 teaspoon vanilla bean paste

2 tablespoons caster (superfine) sugar

600 ml (20½ fl oz) thickened (whipping) cream plus extra, to serve

100 g (3½ oz) white chocolate, chopped

80 ml (2½ fl oz/⅓ cup) good-quality whisky

Pastry

200 g (7 oz/1⅓ cups) plain (all-purpose) flour

55 g (2 oz/¼ cup) caster (superfine) sugar

¼ teaspoon fine sea salt

125 g (4½ oz) cold unsalted butter, cut into 2 cm (¾ in) cubes

2 teaspoons apple cider vinegar mixed with 80 ml (2½ fl oz/⅓ cup) cold water and 4 ice cubes

For the pastry, combine the flour, sugar and salt in a bowl. Add the butter pieces and toss to coat. Turn out onto a clean work surface and, using a pastry cutter (or flat-bladed knife), roughly cut the butter into the flour mixture (leave some large chunks of butter as this will help the pastry to become nice and flaky as it cooks).

Create a well in the centre of the flour mixture and add the vinegar water in 3 batches, working it in with your hands to form a rough dough (you may not need all of the water). Shape into a disc and wrap in plastic wrap. Chill for 3 hours.

Roll out the pastry on a lightly floured work surface to a thickness of 3 mm (⅛ in). Use the pastry to line the base and side of a 22 cm (8¾ in) pie dish then trim the edges. Chill for 30 minutes.

For the custard, whisk together the custard powder, vanilla and sugar in a bowl . Gradually add the cream and keep whisking until smooth. Transfer to a saucepan over medium–low heat and cook, stirring constantly, for 6 minutes or until thick. Remove from the heat and stir in the white chocolate and whisky, beating to combine. Stir until the white chocolate has melted then leave to cool.

Preheat the oven to 200°C (400°F). Line the pastry case with baking paper and fill with baking beads (or uncooked rice or dried beans). Bake for 20 minutes or until the pastry is a light golden colour. Remove the paper and baking beads, then bake for a further 5 minutes or until the base is just dry to the touch.

Remove from the oven and pour the custard filling into the pastry case. Reduce the oven temperature to 140°C (275°F) then bake for 45 minutes or until the custard is set on the edge but still has a wobble in the centre. Cool to room temperature, then chill until cold. Serve with cream.

Yoghurt, walnut and pomegranate pie

When we were coming up with the recipe list for this book, we had really clear ideas of what we wanted to see, but we also asked friends and family what they would expect to see in a book dedicated to sweet pies. They came up with some great ideas on flavours that otherwise may have slipped through the cracks, but also some interesting ideas on how they would like things to look. One night at dinner I asked a good friend Fiona this question and she answered with, 'I'd like to see gold leaf on a pie.' Well, gold leaf turned into silver leaf, and it went perfectly with this Middle Eastern–inspired cold pie. Of course, it's not essential, but the combination of the silver with the pomegranate jewels looks spectacular. – Kirsten

Serves 6

200 g (7 oz) shortbread biscuits (cookies)

100 g (3½ oz/1 cup) toasted walnuts

65 g (2¼ oz) unsalted butter, melted then cooled

2½ titanium-strength gelatine leaves

125 ml (4 fl oz/½ cup) pouring (single/light) cream

80 g (2¾ oz/⅓ cup) caster (superfine) sugar

250 g (9 oz/1 cup) plain Greek-style yoghurt

silver leaf (optional)

seeds from 1 pomegranate to serve

1 tablespoon pomegranate molasses to serve

Pulse the biscuits and walnuts in a food processor to fine crumbs. Add the butter and pulse again to combine. Press the crumb mixture into the base and side of a 17 cm (6¾ in) loose-based fluted tart tin. Chill until needed.

Place the gelatine leaves in a bowl of cold water for 5 minutes to soften. Heat the cream and sugar in a saucepan over medium-low heat to just below boiling point, stirring to dissolve the sugar.

Squeeze any excess water from the gelatine and add the gelatine to the cream mixture, stirring to dissolve. Cool to room temperature, then whisk in the yoghurt until smooth.

Pour the cream mixture into the biscuit base and chill for 3 hours or until firm and set. Decorate with silver leaf (if using) and serve with pomegranate seeds and pomegranate molasses.

Tres leches pie with lime

'Tres leche' translates as 'three milks', and is a traditional Mexican firm sponge cake. The sponge is baked and then soaked in a mixture of condensed milk, evaporated milk and full-cream milk, then chilled. The combination of the three different milks provides a beautiful balance, and the chilled cake is incredibly refreshing in summer. The combination of milks (OK, one of them is cream in our recipe) proves to be just as good in this pie, with the resulting texture being incredibly silky – almost like a cheesecake. Decorate with edible flowers or beautiful seasonal fruit. – Kirsten

Serves 6

445 g (15½ oz) frozen Careme sour cream pastry, thawed, or 1 × portion of pastry from the Spiced apple and golden syrup pie (see page 28), rolled to a thickness of 3 mm (⅛ in)

395 g (14 oz) tin sweetened condensed milk

125 ml (4 fl oz/½ cup) evaporated milk

375 ml (12½ fl oz/1½ cups) pouring (single/light) cream

juice of 2 limes

edible flowers or seasonal fruit, e.g. berries or summer stone fruit, to serve

Use the pastry to line a 29 cm × 14 cm × 5 cm deep (11½ in × 5½ in × 2 in) pie dish, leaving about 2 cm (¾ in) overhang all the way round. Chill for 30 minutes.

Preheat the oven to 200°C (400°F). Line the pastry case with baking paper and fill with baking beads (or uncooked rice or dried beans). Bake for 20 minutes or until the pastry is a light golden colour. Remove the paper and baking beads, then bake for a further 5 minutes or until the base is just dry. Remove from the oven and leave to cool. Reduce the oven temperature to 120°C (250°F).

Whisk together the condensed milk, evaporated milk, cream and lime juice in a bowl. Pour into the pastry case and bake for 1 hour until the edge is set but it still has a gentle wobble in the centre. Cool to room temperature, then chill for 2 hours until cold. Serve with edible flowers or fresh fruit.

LATTICE
how-to

Arrange 4 strips of pastry horizontally on a lightly floured work surface.

Fold back the first and third strips of pastry and place a fifth strip vertically.

Fold every other horizontal strip back on itself and add more vertical strips of pastry, replacing the horizontal strips of pastry between each one.

When all the pastry strips have been used, place over the filling and pinch the edges to seal.

Trim off any excess pastry and discard.

Note: Use a ruler to cut the lattice strips to get a nice straight line.

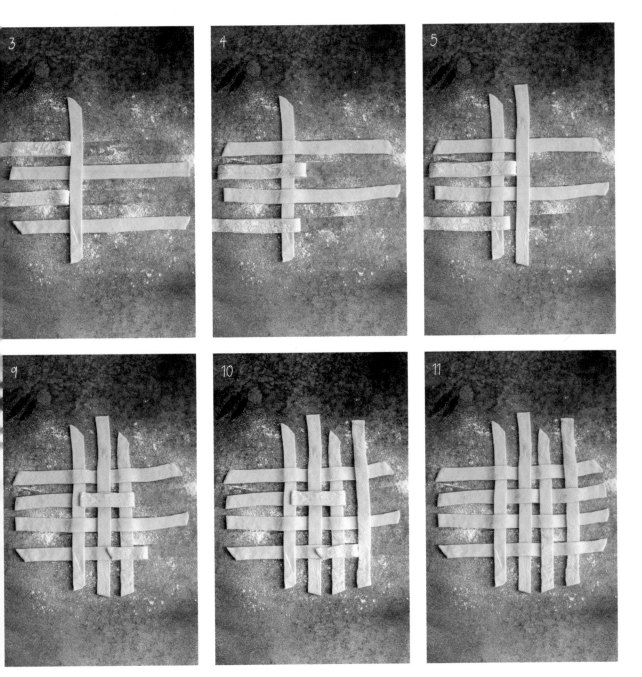

INDEX

ABOUT THE AUTHORS

Phoebe Wood

Phoebe studied Commercial Cookery at TAFE (college) and landed her dream job at *delicious.* magazine at the same time. After four years at *delicious.*, Phoebe left to spend three months in New York gaining inspiration by eating and researching American food. Returning home she worked on a season of *MasterChef Australia* and then landed the position of Food Editor at *SBS Feast* magazine, where she shaped her food philosophy. She has since freelanced across titles such as *MiNDFOOD* and *Prevention* and is now the Senior Food Editor for *delicious.* magazine.

Kirsten Jenkins

After completing Commercial Cookery at TAFE (college), Kirsten spent six months in the UK working on French cookbooks. When she returned to Australia, she was a member of the food team on the first season of *MasterChef Australia* and then worked as a Food Editor at *Donna Hay Magazine* for three years. She has worked on magazines such as *SBS Feast*, *Taste* and *MiNDFOOD*. She is now a freelance recipe developer and food stylist, as well as being Style Editor at *delicious.* magazine.

ACKNOWLEDGEMENTS

Phoebe: This book would not have been possible without the love and support of my partner, Simon. Thank you for listening to me talk incessantly about pies for eight months and for your patience, creative insights and constant encouragement. To my mum and dad, who are my heroes and my inspiration: thank you for raising me to love and care about food, and to be unashamedly creative and carefree with everything I do. To my sisters Grace and Ali, my best friends and my biggest supports, thank you for having really over-the-top reactions every time you eat one of my pies, it makes it all worth it. To my girlfriends Sam, Shannon, Pru and Yasmin, who put their hands up to do some triple-testing, I can't thank you enough for your time. To the *Feast* team, and especially Lara and Anita, who gave me the confidence to believe in myself and my cooking, and who showed me what real food is. Finally, to Kirsten, who is one of the most creatively brilliant people I know. You have been such an inspiration, not just in this pie journey, but since we've met. Your motivation, amazing sense of humour and constant positivity have boosted me throughout this process. Thank you for saying 'yes' to this mad idea, as it could never have happened without you.

Kirsten: First and foremost, I want to thank my beautiful partner, Georgie. I know this has been a crazy year and I know that throwing a book into the mix proved even more crazy! Thank you for your support, guidance, honesty and love! To my mum, dad, Steppy and Kirk, thank you for your love and for constantly reassuring me that I might not be that bad at what I do. To Jody Vassallo, I can't thank you enough for being so generous as to introduce me to the industry and teach me everything you know. To Paula Vassallo, what a bloody good friend you have been. Thank you for always listening and holding my hand when I was occasionally on the edge. To the amazing people I have worked with so far, thank you for pushing me out of my comfort zone and challenging me to do more than I think I can do. And to Phoebe … jeeeezz you're a brilliant friend, work buddy and talent. I could not imagine doing this project with anyone else but you. We made it and I'm so proud of you.

Both: A big thank you to Georgie and Joe at Prop Co-op for finding us pie tins, perfect backgrounds and for pieces that no one else picks up. We can't thank the team at Hardie Grant enough for their support and commitment to our project. To Laura, our wordsmith, who has been so vigilant with every detail in every recipe, and Rachel, our editor, for your support and understanding, and for keeping us on track. Thanks to Courtney, on the other side of the world, for understanding our vision and doing a beautiful job of illustrating it. To Jane and Mark, for your creative vision and belief in us and our idea, thank you for encouraging our project to come to fruition.

Published in 2016 by Hardie Grant Books

Hardie Grant Books (Australia)
Ground Floor, Building 1
658 Church Street
Richmond, Victoria 3121
www.hardiegrant.com.au

Hardie Grant Books (UK)
5th & 6th Floors
52–54 Southwark Street
London SE1 1UN
www.hardiegrant.co.uk

A Cataloguing-in-Publication entry is available from the catalogue
of the National Library of Australia at www.nla.gov.au
The Pie Project
ISBN 978 1 74379 133 2

Publishing Director: Jane Willson
Project Editor: Rachel Day
Editor: Laura Herring
Design Manager: Mark Campbell
Designer: Courtney Eckersley
Typesetter: Patrick Cannon
Photographer: Kirsten Jenkins
Portraits: Simon Kelly
Stylist: Kirsten Jenkins
Production Manager: Todd Rechner

Colour reproduction by Splitting Image Colour Studio
Printed and bound in China by 1010 Printing International Limited

Nutella is a trademark of Ferrero S.p.A.

All recipes in *The Pie Project* use a standard Australian
20 ml tablespoon.